Native Americans
healing powe

G000123407

MOTHER EARTH

PHILIP KUCKUNNIW

Copyright

PHILIP KUCKUNNIW
© Copyright 2020 - All rights reserved.

of the data is without a contract or any guarantee assurance.

The trademarks that are used are without any consent, and the publication of the trademark is without permission or backing by the trademark owner. All trademarks and brands within this book are for clarifying purposes only and are owned by the owners themselves, not affiliated with this document.

The information provided here is correct and reliable, as any lack of attention or other means resulting from the misuse or use of the procedures, procedures or instructions contained therein is the total, and absolute obligation of the user addressed.

The author is not obliged, directly or indirectly, to assume civil or civil liability for any restoration, damage or loss resulting from the data collected here.

The trademarks used are without approval, and the patent is issued without the trademark owner's permission or protection. The logos and labels in this book are the property of the owners themselves and are not associated with this text.

Disclaimer

All intellect contained in this book is given for enlightening and instructive purposes as it were. The creator isn't in any capacity responsible for any outcomes or results that radiate from utilising this material. Worthwhile endeavours have been made to give data that is both precise and viable. However, the creator isn't oriented for the exactness or use/misuse of this data.

Table of Contents

INTRODUCTION

Ten thousand years earlier, when the Ice Age ended, adjustments in the environment and raising populaces motivated some Indigenous American people to experiment with expanding various crops. Some came to be highly competent farmers. Numerous tribes on the coastlines hunted sea mammals from boats and caught fish, using a selection of efficient approaches.

After 2000 BC, some Indigenous Americans established states, each regulating countless people. They established substantial trade routes across the continents. And they utilized cargo rafts and other boats to ship their items from one trading zone to another. In South America, llamas supplied transport ashore.

The Europeans started colonizing the Americas in order to cultivate brand-new farmlands and develop new work for the expanding populations of Europe. To do so, they typically fought Indigenous American tribal countries for the land. Numerous aspects offered the Europeans an advantage in these problems. Initially, they had some resistance to their very own illness. Therefore they were not as ruined by them as Indigenous Americans were. Second, the Europeans had steeds and weapons, which overpowered the Native Americans' hand weapons and arrowheads in battle.

Indigenous American tribal countries withstood emigration, but at some point, lots of them were required to surrender their lands. Present-day southern Canada, the United States, and southern South America, survivors were gathered up and unwillingly transferred to specific areas, called reservations.

In the last few years, growth in transportation and earth-moving equipment has actually made it profitable for outsiders to colonize the tropical lowland woodlands. Currently, the lifestyle for those tribal countries, too, is endangered.

Today Indigenous American populaces across both continents are once more increasing. Native American leaders are accomplishing higher political success in fighting for the rights of their individuals. Furthermore, recent prevalent worry over civil rights has actually triggered federal governments and others to regard Native American cultures and practices when replying to their needs.

Many people are absolutely unaware of the relationship between the onset of illness and the lively underlying changes in their frame's willingness to hold their structures in balance or to combat off invaders that permitted that contamination to take hold. Therefore, they don't comprehend that their state of mind or outlook on existence has an effect on their physical health.

Native individuals trust that healing involves increasing our capability to simply accept lifestyles and let go of ways we have been that has resulted in our imbalanced state. This allows us a risk to make bigger and grow as Souls for most customarily, and it is resistance to alternate and the waft of life activities that have brought on pressure, imbalance, or weak point within the first vicinity.

This manner is regularly invisible to us, however as quickly as we stumble upon a painful occurrence, we will's cope with or recognize physical, emotionally, mentally, or spiritually we get harm, come to be sick, or cut up off a number of our Soul mild and cognizance, which weakens us.

CHAPTER 1 - NATIVE AMERICANS WAY OF LIFE.

The thoughts and perspectives of Native Americans, specifically those who lived during the 15th with 19th centuries, have actually made it through in written kind much less usually than is optimum for the chronicler. Because such documents are incredibly unusual, those thinking about the Native American past attract information from standard arts, folk literature, and folklore.

Native American background is made in complex by the varied geographic and cultural histories of individuals included. As one would certainly anticipate, Native American farmers living in stratified societies, such as the Natchez, engaged with Europeans in a different way than did those who count on hunting and event, such as the Apache.

More-recent events are thought about in the last part of this book, Dope in the late 20th and very early 21st centuries. Figuring out the number of ethnic and political teams in pre-Columbian Northern America is also problematic, not least since meanings of what constitutes an ethnic group or a polity vary with the concerns one looks for.

Ethnic background is most frequently related to some facet of language, while a social or political company can occur on a number of ranges. Therefore, a given collection of people may be defined as an ethnic group through their use of a usual language or language, even as they are recognized as participants of a confederation.

Several other variables including geographical limits, a subsistence base that stressed farming, the visibility or lack of a social or religious power structure, and the inclinations of colonial politicians, among others, likewise impacted ethnic and political category.

The exceptional attribute of North American Indian languages is their diversity-- at contact, Northern America was residence to greater than 50 language households consisting of between 300 and 500 languages. At the exact same minute in the background, western Europe had only two language families (Indo-European and Uralic) and between 40 and 70 languages. To put it simply, if one complies with academic conventions and defines ethnicity through language, Indigenous America was greatly a lot more diverse than Europe.

Politically, most indigenous American groups utilized consensus-based kinds of organization. In such systems, leaders rose in feedback to a specific requirement rather than obtaining some fixed degree of power. No matter the kind of company, however, Native American polities were fairly independent when compared to European areas of comparable dimension.

Over thousands of years, as they moved throughout the continents, American Indians have actually developed a vast array of languages, personalized, and worlds. There are various tribal nations in the Americas as there are nations in Europe, Asia, or Africa, and there is as much variety amongst them.

Native American Wisdom

The words wisdom is utilized frequently each day, whether it is spoken and listened to or written and checked out. Yet it is debatable, in my viewpoint, if most of us know what it is. In many thesauri, it is defined as "the top quality or state of being sensible, sagacious, critical and informative." There are wise people worldwide from all walks of life, from lots of countries and cultures. Yet there is one unalterable fact: No person that is genuinely wise is young.

Likewise, there are numerous old cultures in this world of ours. Therefore, if we widely regard senior citizens as repositories of knowledge, than those old cultures would certainly have much to provide. Lots of indigenous cultures were currently occupying every space and cranny of what we called the United States and Canada when the movement of Europeans started, couple of years back. Those peoples that greeted the novices with varying levels of curiosity and worry had by then survived on this land for thousands upon countless years.

Consequently, they had actually evolved societal values and manner which enabled them not simply to endure, however, grow for all those millennia. Without entering into the unfortunate and difficult details and consequences of the communication between Europeans and native North Americans, it is necessary to keep in mind that the indigenous people were deeply and traumatically affected, to the point where our societies were diminished and in many cases, completely lost. Fortunately is that some of us have survived: simply over 480 ethnically identifiable native people or nations in the America.

A prominent axiom claims that "whatever does not eliminate you will make you more powerful." If that holds true, native cultures have sustained much to survive today, so we must be amongst the toughest people in the world. That stamina is not physical, nevertheless, has nothing to do with army might. That type of toughness has to do with the experiences we had and the insights we acquired from it. Furthermore, everyone as aboriginal cultures and nations are older than anyone of the contemporary nations of North and Central America.

But as I get older, the much more I see the reality in his observation. I understand little of the specific customs, personalized, languages, and values of other native people and nations. What I have discovered is that the foundation of our wisdom is all the truths of the real world. Some are evident: the sunlight comes up in the east and goes down in the west; there are four periods in the yearly cycle winter months, spring, summertime and fall.

Others are a little bit much more refined, however no much less ruthless, such as the knowledge that it is impossible to make it through without knowing those truths and living within them. That is why we did not put our towns on a well-known flood plain, therefore precluding having to blame the river when it flooded. Also, since all our worth's, practices, and personalized care based on truth, the knowledge stemmed from practicing them is real, and not based on myth and legend.

Recovery Powers

The healing customs of Native Americans return for hundreds of years, as the many indigenous people of North America learned that by mixing herbs, origins, and other all-natural plants that they can heal different health troubles. But, treatments were not the only part of the Native American recovery procedure.

With greater than 2,000 people of indigenous tribe in North America, the healing techniques differed commonly from tribe to tribe, entailing various rituals and events. While there were no outright requirements of healing, the majority of tribes believed that wellness was an expression of the spirit and a regular procedure of staying very healthy. This stamina, along with keeping in harmony with themselves, those around them, their native environment, and Designer, would keep away disease and injury.

Everyone was responsible for his or her very own health, and all thoughts and actions had effects, consisting of disease, special needs, misfortune, or injury. Natural solutions filled an important role within these recovery techniques, stretching past the body's pains and discomforts and right into the realm of spirituality and harmony.

The herbs and other all-natural products utilized in treatments were generally gathered from their surrounding setting, causing a wide array of remedies. However, often products that were inaccessible locally were traded over far away. Natural herbs and medicinal plants were typically viewed as deeply spiritual. A number of the different methods have actually been passed down by mouth from generation to generation and never recorded in books, which leaves much of the healing remedies a secret. Just seldom did the healers, such as the Cherokee, that established a composed language, put their formulas or methods in writing.

When very early Europeans arrived in the United States greater than 500 years ago, they were amazed to see Indigenous Americans recovering from diseases and injuries that they took into consideration fatal. In numerous means, the Indians' organic treatments were much above those understood to the brand-new immigrants.

Spirituality and Link:

Then significant difference between Indigenous American recovery and conventional medication, both in the past and existing is their contribution during healing. Native Americans think that all things in nature are linked and that spirits can advertise health and wellness or cause a health problem. Therefore, it is required to heal not just the physical parts of a specific body but their psychological health, and their harmony with their neighbourhood and the environment around them.

Healers

Described as healers, Medication Men, or Medicine woman by their people, they have likewise been called "Shamans" by individuals of European descent. These healers' main duty was to protect the help of the spirit globe, particularly the "Maker" or "Great Spirit," for the advantage of the area or an individual.

The Medicine Man was a clergyman, along with being a medical professional. Believing that condition could be triggered by human, super-ordinary, or all-natural causes, the healer was furnished to treat the ailment in any one of these categories. Masks, which were typically grotesque and horrible, were used by healers to frighten away the spirit triggering the illness or discomfort.

Beating drums and drinking rattles while dancing around the person was likewise made use of to exorcise the devils. The Medicine Man incorporated rights of exorcism with other practical procedures, making use of plant and animal materials.

Constantly an appreciated member of their tribes, being a medicine person was a permanent task, making sure the wellness and balance of both individuals and the tribe itself. In return for his/her solutions, the healer was attended to in all ways, including food, sanctuary, and any help that may be needed. Gifts were provided to the healer for solutions rendered, which might include a wide range of abilities such as natural medication, bone-setting, midwifery, and counselling.

Devices were made use of by the healers which were made from nature, consisting of fur, skins, bone, rocks, coverings, origins, and feathers. In some cases, the healer might go into a hypnotic trance state and seek the assistance of "spirit guides." Acquired problems such as birth defects or retardation were generally not treated. Other problems were also not constantly dealt with if the medical person felt it was the outcome of a person's habits and was a life lesson that needed to be discovered.

Healers maintained their solutions and devices in a medication bundle, made from cloth or hide that was tied safely. There were numerous types of packages the healer's personal bundles, the people's, and bundles made use of for special purposes, such as festivals and events. The contents of each medication package are sacred, and inquiring about the components of a personal package was typically prohibited.

Medication packages coming from people were, in some cases called "grannies," because of the power they held to nourish and support the group. One device frequently located in medication packages is medicine pipes that stand for the ebb and flow of life. It is believed that the breathed out smoke brings prayers as much as the Terrific Spirit.

Healing Rituals and Ceremonies:

Symbolic recovery rituals and events were often held to bring individuals into consistency with themselves, their people, and their environment. Ceremonies were utilized to aid groups of individuals to return to consistency, but not utilized for individual healing. Diverse commonly from tribe to tribe, some people, such as the Sioux and Navajo, made use of a medicine wheel, a spiritual hoop, and would certainly sing and dance in ceremonies that may last for days.

For people, healers could also use dancing, work, altering, drumming, plumes, and rattles in their rituals. For purification and purging, Indigenous Americans typically made use of sweat lodges or sweat baths. Utilized for recovery and harmonizing, it was believed to aid clear evils and rejuvenate the body. These bathrooms can range from just lying under a covering in the hot sunlight, to tiny cone-like structures that were covered by branches and coverings or hides.

Inside the lodge, warm rocks were covered with water to develop a steam bath, and here the healer might pray, sing, or drum together to cleanse the spirits. Sweat lodges were utilized for numerous objectives, occasionally just to help heal an individual, and in some cases, for the majority of individuals before spiritual events or to bring clarity to a problem.

In some cultures, sage, the toughest cleansing natural herb, was melted until it smouldered and gave off clouds of smoke. Called "brushing up the smoke," it was smeared onto the skin and was thought to cleanse the body and soul.

Religion outlawing

Starting in 1882, the Federal government began to function in the direction of prohibiting Native American Religious Legal rights, which impact their medical methods. America Home Secretary Henry M. Bank employee ordered an end to all "heathenish dances and events" on bookings due to their "fantastic obstacle to the world.

These attempts to subdue the traditions of Native Americans ultimately brought about the Carnage at Wounded Knee on December 29, 1890, when the federal government attempted to stop the technique of the "Ghost Dancing," a far getting to motion that forecasted a relaxed end to white American growth and taught goals of clean living, a straightforward life, and cross-cultural participation by Native Americans.

When the Seventh United State Calvary was sent right into the Lakota Sioux's Pine Ridge and Rosebud Reservations to quit the dancing and apprehend the participants about 150 Native American men, ladies, and youngsters were eliminated.

Though costs of killing innocents were brought versus members of the Seventh Calvary, all were vindicated. Simply two years later on, more steps were required to reduce Native faiths when Commissioner of Indian Affairs Thomas J. Morgan ordered penalties of up to 6 months in prison for those who repeatedly participated in spiritual dances or worked as medicine men. Nevertheless, these new regulations were virtually difficult to enforce, and the Native Americans continued their customs.

Before 1900, Native Americans depended upon their medication, people for all illness and injury. Nevertheless, that started to change in the early 20th century as hospitals and facilities were opened by the Indian Health Service. Remarkably, the ban of Native American spiritual rituals remained to be in place until the 1978 flow of the American Indian Religious Flexibility Act.

Regrettably, as a result of the years of the restriction, many Native American recovery techniques were driven underground or lost totally.

Today, several tribes remain to safeguard the expertise of their medication men and will not go over the topic with non-Indians.

For hundreds of years, Native Americans have used herbs not just to recover the body, yet to cleanse the spirit and bring equilibrium right into their lives and their environments. While there were numerous herbs and plants used in Native American remedies, one of the most spiritual was Tobacco, which was utilized to recovery countless problems, as well as in rituals and events.

One more really vital natural herb to the Native Americans was Sage, which was stated to not only heal numerous issues of the stomach, colon, kidneys, liver, lungs, skin, and a lot more, it was thought to protect against bad spirits and to draw them out of the body or the soul.

Though the checklist of natural medicinal herbs that could be lugged in a Therapist's medication package are several and differed, those that were most often used were regularly lugged such as remedies for colds which could consist of American Ginseng or Boneset; herbs for aches and discomforts consisting of Wild Black Cherry, Pennyroyal, and treatments for high temperature, including Dogwood, Feverwort, and Willow Bark.

Native Americans Rituals

The thoughts and perspectives of aboriginal people, specifically those that lived throughout the 15th through 19th centuries, have endured in written kind much less commonly than is ideal for the chronicler. Due to the fact that such records are extremely unusual, those curious about the Native American past draw information from typical arts, folk literature, folklore and lot more.

Native American history is made furthermore complex by the diverse geographic, and cultural histories of the peoples entailed as one would expect, native American farmers, staying in stratified societies, such as the Natchez, involved with Europeans in different ways than did those that depend on searching and celebration, such as the Apache. Likewise, Spanish vanquishers were taken part in a basically various kind of colonial venture than were their equivalents from France or England.

Ethnic background is most often equated with some facet of language, while the social or political company can happen on a variety of ranges simultaneously. Thus, a provided collection of people might be specified as an ethnic group with their use of a common dialect or language also as they are recognized as participants of embedded polities such as a clan, a town, and a confederation.

Other elements, consisting of geographical boundaries, a subsistence base that emphasized either foraging or farming, the existence or lack of a social.

The superior feature of North American Indian languages is their diversity-- at getting in touch with Northern America was home to greater than 50 language family members. At the exact same minute in history, western Europe had just two language family members (Indo-European and Uralic) and between 40 and 70 languages. Simply put, if one adheres to academic conventions and specifies ethnic culture through language, Native America was vastly extra diverse than Europe.

Politically, most Native American teams made use of consensus-based kinds of organization. In that kind of organization, leaders rose in response to a specific need as opposed to getting some set level of power. The Southeast Indians and the Northwest Coastline Indians were exemptions to this basic regulation, as they most regularly stayed in ordered societies with a clear primary class. Despite the type of company, however, indigenous American polities were quite independent when compared with European communities of comparable size.

Years before, Christopher Columbus stepped foot on what would become referred to as the Americas, and the extensive territory was occupied by Native

Americans. Throughout the 16th and 17th centuries, as even more explorers looked for to colonize their land, Native Americans responded in numerous stages, from teamwork to indignation to revolt.

After exterior siding with the French in various battles during the French and Indian War and becoming forcibly gotten rid of their residences under Andrew Jackson's Indian Removal Act, Native American populations were decreased in size and region by the end of the 19th century. Christopher Columbus arrives on a Caribbean Island after three months of taking a trip. Believing at first that he had actually reached the East Indies, he defines the natives he meets as "Indians." On his very first day, he orders six natives to be seized as servants.

Over hundreds of years, as they migrated across the continents, American Indians have created a wide variety of languages, custom-made, and worlds. There are as various tribal nations in the Americas as there are countries in Europe, Asia, or Africa, and there is as much range amongst them.

Ten thousand years earlier, when the Glacial period ended, modifications in climate and enhancing populaces inspired some Native American tribes to try out expanding various plants. Some ended up being highly skilled farmers. Many tribes on the coasts pursued sea animals from watercraft and captured fish, making use of a selection of efficient approaches.

After 2000 BC, some Native Americans created states, each governing hundreds of people. They established extensive trade routes throughout the continents. And they made use of cargo rafts and various other watercraft to ship their products from one trading point to one more.

From the present-day region of the mid-western USA to southern Peru in South America, facilities of government were marked by enormous mounds of earth. Most of these mounds were level ahead, with palaces and holy places improved them. Some were burial grounds of honoured leaders.

European intrusions of the Americas began with Columbus's trips to the "New World" in 1492. The Europeans brought illness with them, including smallpox and measles. These unknown conditions spread swiftly among Native Americans. They erased the populations of lots of native cities.

The Europeans began conquering the Americas in order to cultivate brand-new farmlands and produce brand-new work for the expanding populace of Europe. To do so, they frequently dealt with Native American tribal nations for the land. Several elements gave the Europeans the benefit of these problems.

Initially, they had some resistance to their own diseases. European negotiations in the Americas grew at such a rate that the Europeans' descendants at some point exceeded the native individuals.

Native American tribal nations withstood colonization, but ultimately, many were required to surrender their lands. - contemporary southern Canada, the United States, and southerly South America, survivors were gathered up and unwillingly moved to particular areas, called reservations. In the last couple of years, advancements in transport and earth-moving machinery have actually made it lucrative for outsiders to conquer the exotic lowland area.

Today Native American populaces throughout both continents are once more on the rise. Native American leaders are achieving higher political success in defending the legal rights of their individuals. In addition, recent prevalent worry over civil rights has triggered federal governments and others to respect Native American cultures and customs when responding to their needs.

Shamans and medicine men

Native American Indians sought spiritual recommendations and healing from the drugs individual in their tribe. These religious healers had a deeply sacred connection to all of the factors of nature. They were visible as mystics, prophets, and teachers.

Incredibly respected by way of all in their tribesmen, medicinal drug males and females achieved rituals containing chants, smudging, and symbolic dance. These rituals were used to solve any imbalance between top and evil that can exist in the tribe at a given time. The Native Americans believed strongly that awful spirits had been the reason for sickness, dying, and discourse within their people.

Remedy men might turn to their medicine bag, and its contents to treat anything was ailing a member of their tribe. Gadgets found on this sacred bag are nevertheless used these days in rituals and spiritual ceremonies. Things like candy grass braids, witch hazel bark, white sage, Echinacea, and incense have been all quintessential elements in the healing rituals performed by using the medicine women and men.

In the local American Indian subculture, a few healers also had the ability to result in visions. These humans were known as shamans. The maximum skilled of all healers, the tribal shaman, became capable of input a deep trance that connected them to the underworld searching for recovery. Those bright and severe desires added the shaman to a better state of reality.

It changed into believed that in this heightened country, the barrier among humans and animals changed into blurred, and they may speak with one another. The religious journeys that shaman travelled on had been thought to attach them to the spiritual courses that presented them information and insight into the desires of their tribesmen. Every shaman could have a spirit animal that they related to and that protected them on their voyage through attention.

The Native American Indians have a deeply rooted notion in nature and spirituality that is both beautiful and profound. Their connection to all matters - residing and non-living, massive and small, is inspiring and honourable. If you have a curiosity or interest in performing the rituals of the local American humans, these products can help you with your journey.

CHAPTER 2 – HISTORIC RECOVERY OF NATIVE AMERICANS

The word "healing" is used in many approaches; however, to the Native American, it's miles greater than just avoiding invading disease. However, it takes into consideration that our bodies are not cut loose by our thoughts, emotions, or soul. Because of this, healing takes on deeper, which means inside the local American traditions.

Many people are absolutely unaware of the relationship between the onset of illness and the lively underlying changes in their frame's willingness to hold their structures in balance or to combat off invaders that permitted that contamination to take hold. Therefore, they don't comprehend that their nation of mind or outlook on existence has an effect on their physical health as a lot, if now not extra than what they consume or how a lot they sleep.

We can change the manner we view healing and weave back recovery, like an exquisite tapestry torn by means of time and trauma that has been stained or abused. It takes more than easy maintenance or closing up of holes to return to its original splendour.

While the frame is vulnerable or ill more is wanted than chemical treatments to kill germs or idiot unbalanced stems. Rebalancing and reunification of all aspects of the Self are needed to fix and reweave our active structures desires to take the region to reconnect the shredded fibres of the body, thoughts, feelings, and the soul. Proper healing is gaining the balance of what we are, how we think, what we experience, what we do, and how we stay on all levels of our lives concurrently.

Native individuals trust that healing involves increasing our capability to simply accept lifestyles and let go of ways we have been that has resulted in our imbalanced state. This allows us a risk to make bigger and grow as Souls for most customarily, and it is resistance to alternate and the waft of life activities that have brought on pressure, imbalance, or weak point within the first vicinity.

This manner is regularly invisible to us, however as quickly as we stumble upon a painful occurrence, we will's cope with or recognize physical, emotionally, mentally, or spiritually we get harm, come to be sick, or cut up off a number of our Soul mild and cognizance, which weakens us.

If we are willing to do the works to appearance actually interior of ourselves, face something illness or trauma, learn from it, and permit healing exchange, we are able to regain our Soul light and focus. We also can evolve our Souls through this procedure and obtain what we name "fitness."

Almost every person has unresolved bodily, emotional, intellectual, or non-secular troubles, some of which we are completely unaware of or in denial about. But, take into account that everybody can enjoy the tactics of healing as a way to clear up these troubles and move to better recognition.

Real recovery is an exploration of self-discovery and an opportunity for personal enlightenment that we can all gain from. It takes braveness to take for your personal healing, but by means of doing so, you will embark on a manner of transformation in order to enlarge your thoughts, coronary heart, and soul.

Native Americans accept as true with that something can be healed, inclusive of our potential to heal ourselves. However, every now and then we need extra energy, extra knowledge, or greater love than we are able to muster all by means of ourselves to gain it.

These are the times while we should be willing to simply accept the help from others, whether they are the circle of relatives, friends, or trained specialists skilled in the healing arts if we without a doubt do want healing to arise, for we are not here to heal alone.

Every folk is made up of many elements and on many stages. A few are dense and bodily even as others are higher in vibration. Our minds and feelings are collections of swimming patters of strength, emotions, thoughts, and attention that in no way prevent. These fragments of identification are linked with our physicality and rule over our physical capabilities, but on occasion, seem to exist in their own private world. At the very best stage, we are pure power and spirit.

It's far-right here that we see the components of ourselves that are metaphysical, which go past the realm of depending and intertwine with different people, dimensions, and the general focus or God. Of all of these ranges, it's miles through the mind that we have got right of entry to the maximum strength, for through concept and awareness, we can create or destroy the sensitive balances that exist between us and the out of doors international.

What might you be like in case you were whole? If you recognize precisely who you are, wherein you got here from, and what you are right here on earth to do, who might you feel? Tapping into these inner sources to do something you selected and do and calmly succeeding at it's far what healing is all about. What would it be want to experience ideal, sturdy fitness, and complete peace on your thoughts and emotions?

We speak to me about regaining the factors of ourselves which have to emerge as shut down, break up off, or suppressed to the pint that we experience misplaced, weak, incapable, irritated, depressed, powerless, or simply simple ill. This fragmentation diffuses our power and interest and reasons us to be not able to completely have interaction in life the way we must be capable of, not to mention the manner we dream of.

For lots of us, this breaking apart of the Self may have commenced early on in life or so long as we will consider, that have felt like chains that maintain us returned from our coronary heart's dreams. We aren't breaking away our thoughts, emotions, and religious our bodies, therefore that's why we have to heal all aspects of ourselves at the same time as supporting, guiding, and even challenging ourselves as we walk down the course to recovery.

We at Holistic Bodyworks works with those ancient teachings and strategies to help our clients gain the balance they want to bring about the health of mind, body, and soul. As healers and teachers, how can we help you? First of all, we listen in your story and come up with options, for this is frequently why human beings sense caught. Maximum customers were invested in a healthcare gadget that doesn't serve their desires and gainer's pay for an alternative, which results in feeling that no person is aware of the way to assist them.

We help people grow into true fitness with supportive steering and strategies that use just the proper mix of intuition, emotional, metaphysical, physical, and non-secular schooling, power and vocational recovery techniques, listening, speak remedy, coaching, and religious recovery.

We will "maintain area" and energy for you, supporting you hold the focus of vintage physical, emotional, mental, non-secular, familial, ancestral, and beyond life energies and styles as collectively we creatively ruin them up, reform them, and reintegrate them into a brand new, healthier and happier you.

In the quick run, we'll help you are taking stock of your existence and study your body, health conduct, thoughts, emotions, relationships, work state of affairs, and private goals. We'll then offer new and practicable opportunities for adjustments you could make in those areas. We'll use our intuitive abilities to assess your bodily, emotional, mental, and spiritual structures and support them with palms-on recovery as needed.

In the long run, we'll be your instructors, coaches, and cheerleaders as you undergo your own private transformation, for authentic healing isn't always in reality recovery of the body, but a process of turning into something new.

Typically, it isn't affordable to unravel and fix an entire life of physical, mental, emotional, and non-secular clutter in only one consultation. You didn't get to where you are in a single day; however, through years of accrued physical and emotional assaults.

It can take many sessions over a period of time to get sufficient predominant issues resolved to be robust sufficient to make the important changes for properly. That is where the patience and determination of both healer and seeker are had to deliver resolution ultimately.

In any other case, it will take lots longer for any medical doctor or healer to assist. Considered one of our major desires is to assist human beings to understand this very truth and take lower back their personal power to heal themselves. After they do, they will keep in mind that they have constantly been on top of things of their own lives and fitness, whether they know it consciously or now not.

Healing the body and soul

Over 10,000 years ago, the ancestors of Native American tribes commenced supplying stones to the frame for natural recovery and wellness. Stone medication applies these ancient traditions in ceremonies the usage of healing stones, gem and stone stones, and various animal 'drug treatments' or energies and natural drug treatments to heal the spirit body, emotional, & bodily body. The strategies of Stone medicinal drugs assist the body in self-healing and are not just supposed to return to the physical body to well-being, however the emotions and the spirit as properly.

Through clearing the body of negative energies and reconnecting it to the healing energies of the earth, the frame's ability to heal itself is re-established. Those imprints or resonance patterns propel our life in a sure path through attracting human beings, situations, and reviews to us.

Humans regularly blame the instances in their beginning for his or her modern-day lifestyles. However, we've seen, in infinite public figures, the strength to triumph over their deep traumas and wreck through the chances into the existence of untamed fulfilment. It's crucial to understand that those public figures had been as soon as just like us, regular human beings with struggles and goals, facing obstacles.

In shamanic healing traditions, feelings are considered as energies and they're understood through the Shamans and used as effective energies to perform many dreams. Emotions are valued as tools that are particular to human beings, with which they can show up new realities.

Each negative and wonderful emotions can be utilized. The enjoyment of worry, as an example, offers us and possibility to confront, renowned, and remodel our boundaries. And while we experience the love we turn out to be effective beyond degree. Folks who feel love and provide love are capable of acquiring love to go back and are in a position to accomplish any intention.

By releasing our terrible patterns or emotions through Stone medication and historical earth primarily based health practices and integrating new imprints, you'll be in a position to interrupt free of old styles and consciously create your life from the location of clarity, fluidity, abundance, pleasure, and success.

Shamanic healing is primarily based on love and compassion and it really works for our whole and total wellbeing: mental, emotional, spiritual and bodily. When you recode the limiting patterns you've inherited or imprinted through poor reports, you are making way for new studies, and open to effective, effective effects. Those traditional native practices are used that will help you heal and recognize the means of your existence.

The spiral is a universally normal image of eternity, and in some traditions, it symbolizes the power of all creation. While the spiral is used to make the form of a hand, the resulting parent is assumed to be infused with therapeutic power. The Healer's Hand is an ancient symbol of healing and safety, and it's far taken into consideration to be representative of the healing powers of healing hands.

Healing hands or Waphiyapi Nape is a term used to describe a historic wellness approach taught to "healers," for the duration of the local American countries. Healers were supplying this form of fingers-on, lively recovery for generations. The most commonplace shape of these works in our cutting-edge profession is referred to as Reiki.

Recovery palms use a special symbol device than Reiki but draw at the equal innate knowledge of the universe to result from instability for the customer. The symbols utilized in healing fingers were drawn as Petroglyphs and Pictographs in local American rock artwork during the Americas.

You may have attempted traditional remedy and now not experienced the kind of effects which you have been hoping for. You could find yourself stuck within the same self-defeating patterns yr. after year. Whether you're fighting with melancholy, or being known as to clear unhealthy styles, and obtain freedom out of your beyond traumas, or you desire to be more fulfilled and convey your desires into reality, shamanic practices have served our health for thousands of years.

Healers believe there are two kinds of ailments. Some can be created through our day by day behaviour or behaviour and a few which can be our own family, surroundings, or socially and spiritually related. All illnesses may be associated with strength on the religious level and may, therefore, be converted with energy medicinal drug practices. The trendy knowledge in neuroscience, biology, and functional medicinal drug validate the profound and lasting outcomes you can gain with energy healing practices.

Maximum depressed and hectic humans are greater liable to contamination & terrible energies, which can create a cyclical effect that feels by no means ending. Love, information, and compassion are key for the hit recovery of despair, sickness, & illness: mental, emotional, or bodily.

These healing immersions provide you maps to navigate and tools to find the courage, power and imaginative and prescient to discover and alternate the styles and ideals keeping you from dwelling the existence you choice. During the in-depth personal consultation, we unwind a selected sample or difficulty and create a brand new cognizance to propel you forward with clarity and reason.

Get to the bottom of the tales and release the fears around difficult life transitions, acquire clear sight and remove the filters of your belief to transport forward. Reprogram your power discipline and brain pathways. Reconnect in your mind innermost knowing and anchor your visions into your body. Enjoy historical rite and acquire healing for difficult life transitions, healing from grief, and gain readability for life cause.

Inyan Pejuta or Stone medication is a Native American recovery art combining traditional ceremonies, herbal drug treatments, and stone medicinal drug treatments to assist your healthy and tremendous recovery. This will resource in new beginnings and alignment with soul reason, will also help to cleanse and detoxify the frame, mind, spirit, and soul.

One of the remedies you may experience is called the Rain bath ceremony. Rain bath rite is a historical shape of thoughts frame health in which natural medication is blended with healing stones, supposed to rebalance the physical and emotional our bodies through affecting the frightened machine with plant oils and stones of diverse temperatures. A ramification of emotional and bodily ailments may be stricken by the natural medicines (energies) used at some stage in a Rain bath session.

For those looking for a greater connection to the which means of life and needing wellbeing for the thoughts, body, and spirit personalized character retreats serve to encourage clearly life converting reviews focused on your individual wellbeing dreams. Those non-public and customized retreats provide the perfect set of studies that will help you clean the beyond and flow ahead, empower yourself, and assist you to sense connected, clean, and complete.

Preventive Measures

First-rate Lakes tribes hired a diffusion of defensive or preventive measures towards contamination; some had been the person and some were institution efforts. Native human beings did now not distinguish between medicinal drugs, in the clinical or scientific sense, and charms. In fact, the Ojibwe time period for remedy, muski'ki, covered each class. Charms are the one's matters which affect both human beings and nature without real touch or ingestion, at the same time as medicines are substances that are administered at once to a person for healing.

Charms

Charms, like medication, had been almost usually bought from every other man or woman and have been the method of assuring true fortune in searching, fishing, trapping, playing, conflict, and love. Also, they covered the people from sickness or physical damage. Although charms may be used for malevolent functions, the vast majority were concerned with the food quest, specifically hunting.

In maximum times, the allure was carried in a small deerskin packet on the character. Love charms and those for use for malicious rationale have been normally stored within the domestic rather than worn at the frame.

Dream Fetishes

Dream fetishes had been sacred private articles one retained in the course of lifestyles, and which guarded towards damage or misfortune. They will be received because of the result of a dream of a near relative or namesake who may also have presented the article to a man or woman in infancy or formative years. Dream fetishes may also originate through the work of the drugs guy at some stage in the shaking tent ritual.

Those items have been given unique care and dealing with and have been held on the hoop of a toddler's cradleboard or over the bed of a grownup. They had been retained for life and, if accidentally destroyed or wiped out, were changed with a counterpart. These articles were taken to spiritual ceremonies, carried on long journeys, and buried with the individual at their demise.

Tobacco Services

Tobacco offerings to the thunderbirds have been a commonplace approach of securing protection against belongings damage and bodily injury during a windstorm. When a storm got here up, tobacco becomes located on a stump within the backyard or a pinch of tobacco become thrown into the fire. In a few cases, the person spoke to the thunderbirds, asking for safety. However, this becomes now not important; the offering itself turned into enough.

Avoiding Taboos

Some other manner of maintaining character health was by means of faithfully watching certain taboos. In a few instances, the breach of taboo affected the transgressor, however extra frequently, it led to harm to a person else. Most taboos did not challenge health, however, breaking menstrual and mourning taboos may want to cause bodily harm or loss of life. Local humans believed that touch with a menstruating girl or whatever she touched was rather dangerous.

Girls received instructions regarding this taboo throughout puberty fast on the time of their first menstruation period. They were being kept hidden in a special hut for every week or extra, at some point in which they have been delivered meals but cooked it themselves on their personal fireplace, and ate it in unique dishes reserved for this purpose. They were warned now not to wash inside the lake for fear of killing the rice crop. A menstruating girl turned into never to step over a young baby or over a man's garb, for sickness or maybe dying may want to result.

A person in mourning became now not allowed to touch children until after the removal-of-Mourning rite. Throughout this era, the mourner's touch should produce illness or cause the loss of life of a baby.

Retaining network fitness

There were also unique methods of shielding the fitness of a whole community or an individual. Among the Wisconsin Ojibwe, approaching illness can be warded off with the aid of destroying a straw man built to represent the threatening contamination or malevolent pressure. If a person turned into warned by means of his father or mother spirit that disorder or contamination become - to strike the community, he sent out a runner.

Tobacco turned into the way of inviting people to those unique feasts, and the runner provided each family with a piece of tobacco and advised them while and in which to collect and to bring materials to make a photo. On the appointed time, the humans appeared with food and tobacco, the guys carrying weapons, the ladies and youngsters with knives, clubs, and axes.

The dreamer associated his dream and explained why he had referred to as them collectively. Food was laid out on the ground, and tobacco was passed around and smoked even as the dreamer devoted both meals and tobacco to the manidog, asking their blessing at the lawsuits.

Both the food, because it changed into being eaten, and the tobacco, in the shape of smoke, determined their manner to the spirits. Then the people, wearing their weapons, went outdoors and cautiously approached the straw guy -- made by way of the runner or by the ladies -- which have been set up by using the runner a quick distance from the house.

The parent -- two to 4 feet in height and wearing miniature male clothing -- became built out of straw or hay so it would burn. Because the crowd approached the straw guy, the dreamer gave the sign for the guys to shoot it, and he joined them.

The girls and kids also rushed up to membership it, cut it, and chop it to bits. The stays have been accumulated up, either with the aid of the group or the runner, located in a pile and burned. The dreamer then thanked the entire meeting for their assistance.

Any other group tries to beat back coming near disaster was through the technique of the "imparting tree." An individual might be warned with the aid of his guardian spirit that sickness turned into - to descend on the community. Invitational tobacco was carried to some of the humans by the runner, who knowledgeable them wherein and while to bring together. At the appointed time they could come, bringing food, tobacco, and articles of garb.

The food turned into unfolding out and the tobacco handed, both of them being supplied to the manidog of the air, especially the thunderbirds. This was executed with the aid of the dreamer or by a person he targeted to talk to him. The dreamer related his dream and instructed the manidog that this offering of apparel was of their honour and implored their intercession in fending off the illness.

After the feast, the garb and tobacco brought by way of the participants had been tied close to the top of a tree, a post leaned up against the residence, or a put up set upright on the floor.

The apparel was presupposed to be the one's items worn close to the frame, consisting of underwear, pants, shirts, clothes, and aprons. They were to be left putting for at the least four days, for the duration of which they had been time-honoured by using the manidog. After that, they were used as dishrags or, in some cases, they had been allowed to stay till they disintegrated.

Every now and then, a special dance known as the courageous or leader Dance observed the ceremony of clothes placing and was supposed to enlist the guardian spirits of a number of human beings to assist one or more individuals or the complete network. This became the equal dance used before warfare to muster protective forces.

Curative treatments

In case of injury, fractured limbs were certain with basswood cords to splints made of cedar or heavy birch bark. Other surgical strategies covered enamel extraction. Superb Lakes Indians also employed three different strategies of mechanical curing, inclusive of cupping, "tattooing," and the sweat bathtub.

Cupping

"Cupping" is a term for the exercise in any other case referred to as "bleeding" because it turned into practiced historically through Euro-American physicians. There's no archaeological evidence to prove its use prehistorically, but it's tremendously huge distribution among local individuals strongly suggests a local starting place.

Usually, cupping practitioners have been girls (in Ojibwe, actually reducing or scratching girls), and there had been no cult or supernatural strategies linked with it. An apprentice should gather the method and knowledge for a price. The patient gave the physician a fee, tobacco, and one common article, which includes a blanket. The maximum common illnesses treated by means of cupping had been complications and blood poisoning, but it was extensively utilized for dizziness, pain, swelling, and rheumatism. The gadget consisted of a sharp instrument for making the incision and a section of horn.

The cupping device turned into made from the small end of a cow's horn, 3 or 4 inches long, which were wiped clean out and the end perforated. To cure a headache, the physician made a slanting incision inside the affected person's temple to strike a vein. She then placed the massive cease of the horn reduce after which sucked at the small stop to draw off the blood, which was stuck in a dish. It became emptied outside in an isolated spot in which no person might step on it or disturb it.

Bloodletting became restrained to the head and limbs. For blood poisoning, the individual becomes bled until "all the dark blood became out and the blood ran crimson and clean." a local astringent changed into employed to stop the bleeding, and a few doctors carried out a native salve to the cut after the bleeding had stopped. In a few cases or three treatments over a length of several weeks had been essential before a treatment changed into finished.

"Tattooing"

"Tattooing" become some other method for treating the identical ailments as had been dealt with by way of cupping. The term tattooing is rather deceptive. However, it's far the one native people used themselves when referring to this kind of cure in English. Individual professionals (generally women) laboured without supernatural help for a fee of tobacco plus a blanket or beadwork.

Traditionally, the tattooing tool became either the higher or decrease jaw of a garfish, which had long rows of needle-like teeth. Medication becomes constantly implemented together with tattooing, regularly inside the shape of a poultice. The instrument becomes first dipped into a native medicine, then "hammered" onto the sore spot. The cause of the tattooing becomes to pierce the pores and skin so the drugs would penetrate the blood circulate. The pain experienced in the course of the treatment turned into the discomfort, leaving the body.

Sweat Baths

The sweat bathtub became used by nearly all North American tribes and extended as a long way south as Guatemala. The leader motive of the sweat bath was healing, even though it performed a distinguished function within the ritual of the Midewiwin as well as being taken even as on the hunt to take away doors which recreation could recognize. Sweat baths have been used to all through the colds, fevers, and rheumatism. The sweat motel changed into a small wigwam just massive enough for one character and absolutely blanketed with birch bark or blankets.

While it became completed, heated stones have been carried inner. The patient, who changed into stripped, created steam by way of sprinkling water on the stones with a group of grass or cedar boughs. The water from time to time contained medication or could be used on my own. After the tub, the affected person was rubbed down, wrapped up, and put to the mattress.

Besides the sweating tub, different types of remedy had also been inhaled in steam or smoke. For rheumatism, a hole changed into dug in the ground to maintain a kettle containing the herbal medicinal drug for rheumatism steeped in hot water.

Remedy men

An awful lot of the healing characteristic in the conventional woodland way of life became delegated to the medication person. For wooded areas, Indians, fitness, and long existence represented the best top and those who possessed expertise conducive to that quit changed into the maximum.

The primary, the "tent-shaker" and the "sucking health practitioner," loved extraordinarily excessive fame and were normally the maximum feared and revered individuals in the community because they possessed and could exercise power to practice evil as well as appropriate. The 1/3 type, the Wabeno (actually "Morning superstar man" in Menominee), derived his strength from the Morning big name, which turned into much less than benevolent.

Despite the fact that their powers had been received at some stage in the imaginative and prescient quest throughout their teenagers, they remained inactive until pretty overdue in lifestyles. They could not practice until centre age or later as it was stated that if newbie medicinal drug mans started out too early, they might forfeit their energy or even their lives.

A few individuals combined each of the shaking tent and sucking physician roles. The shaking tent medical doctor had wider powers, consisting of recovery magically and possessing a clairvoyant potential to determine reasons for infection, including sorcery and breach of taboo.

Sucking Docs

The sucking physician laboured to take away the cause of illness through sucking it out of the affected person's body. After he had widely wide-spread the initial gift of tobacco that constituted a request for remedy, the medical doctor stipulated the time, the region, and the fee of the ceremony. The ceremonies normally have been held within the night-time or at night time, and a small institution of witnesses had been a gift.

The organization might encompass the health practitioner, his assistant or runner, the affected person, and some spectators, regularly friends or household of the patient.

In greater latest times, the tubes were brass cartridge cases with the ends removed. The patient, typically partially stripped, became stretched out at the ground on a blanket. Tobacco turned into handed, and anyone could take a pinch. The health practitioner dedicated the tobacco to the spirits and enlisted their aid. All the while, he shook his rattle and turned into observed by way of the assistant's drumming.

With the tube projecting from his mouth, he kneeled over the affected person, moving about till he placed the place wherein the sickness originated, sucked out the object through the tube, and spit both it and the tube into the shallow dish.

The drumming ceased, and the dish turned into handed around for inspection. Numerous such sucking may occur earlier than any depend become seen within the dish. A curing ritual would possibly be closing from a half-hour to 2 hours, depending upon the achievement or wishes of the health practitioner.

Shaking Tent

The shaking tent health practitioner used a unique tent or wigwam. While it varies quite in form and production, it becomes basically a pole framework about three feet in diameter and 7 feet high. The cylindrical facets have been protected with skins, birch bark, or blankets to conceal the drugs guy.

However, the dome-shaped top was left exposed. The conjuror called on positive supernatural spirits to return into the tent and they entered through the uncovered top. The most essential of these changed into the turtle, which became also big to the Waban, who hung the dried shell of a snapping turtle from his tambourine drum.

When the spirits entered the tent, it'd shake violently. The magician consulted with these spirits, every of which had a specific voice understandable only to the medicine man. The spirits provided the statistics necessary to remedy problems along with the area of lacking people or lost articles and the supply of disorder, such as whether the disease became natural or had supernatural reasons such as sorcery, spirit intrusion, sickness-object intrusion, breach of taboo, or soul loss.

With this information, the medicine man may want to prescribe a treatment or bypass information that could assist solve the purchaser's hassle. The medicine guy could also release the spirit from his own body and send it off to examine what brought about the illness in one in every one of his sufferers.

Wabeno

The Wabeno also executed his energy during the days of his early imaginative and prescient quest, but extra regularly used it to inflict harm. The Wabeno changed into also on occasion visible at night inside the guise of a fireball. Due to his information on plant life and their houses, he became consulted to reap looking charms and love charms. Love charms had been intended to attract and keep the attention of a member of the opposite intercourse who would possibly otherwise not be fascinated.

Medicinal drug men used a spread of fetishes, and gadgets thought to possess the paranormal energy to result in precise consequences. Generally, these have been collectible wood figurines in human shape, and inside super Lakes tribes, human snapshots have been seldom made for every other reason. For love magic -- to attract an accomplice or keep a wedding collectively -- the medication man used a male and a girl figure and bound them collectively.

In a few wood figures, a hollow space changed into cut within the chest to maintain magical items, such as smaller collectible figurines. Those could be used to reinforce fitness or result in contamination. If a man or woman suspected that a medicinal drug man became running evil in opposition to him, he would possibly engage another medicinal drug guy to counteract it.

Exactly while you are taking your first step, you're making a deep reference to the Earth, our mother, the energy of mother Earth pulls you closer to each other. Each time your eyes take one blink mother, Earth gives you a special present to see on every occasion. The bark of trees on how each stem has a hidden photograph in it, even as the leaves have shifting hues in them. Stepping even in the direction of that tree, you give it a tree hug, sending the message to the tree that you love him.

Slowly leaves start falling in the path of you, sending a message from the tree announcing that he loves you too. Receiving the message, you set one leaf for your hand at the identical time as feeling mother Earth's heartbeat. You step lower back on course, knowing every tree can be a habitat to a chunk wild creature, clearly as you have got your private habitat.

As you maintain walking, the connection with mother Earth courses you to appearance up to the sky. The shapes of clouds within the sky have meaning to every one among them. Mother Earth continually has a hidden pattern inside the clouds of her wild animals. We're all given our very own religious present from mother Earth, so we all see distinctive. As soon as we've got observed that gift from mother Earth, the wind will slowly shape distinctive figures within the clouds.

When you preserve following your course, you look up to the clear blue sky and spot a hawk sailing through the sky. Depending on what you do on your lifestyles, that message from mother Earth may have a one of a kind which means to absolutely everyone.

Having found out that water is mother Earth's blood, the rocks are her bones, and the land is her pores and skin. Together with your ears, you start listening to sounds of strolling water and that sound pulls you in. Your eyes make a stable photo of mother Earth and store it on your reminiscence and you may in no manner overlook it.

Listening to the night-time birds start to sing, mother Earth informs you that your journey is coming to a resting point. Calmingly on foot deeper into the timber, you begin accumulating sticks and stones and setting stone facet with the aid of facet forming into the shape of a circle, the shape of mother Earth. You location your eyes at the hearth, and spot the smoke start to form. Inside the smoke above the fireplace, you begin to see spiritual animals emplaced among it.

While you start seeing all the spiritual animals take shape, you furthermore may see first nations begin dancing around a fire. Looking deep into the fireplace, the means being instructed became of a first nation having a rain dance. Even as mother Earth become supplying you with a night display, the northern lighting had taken location within the sky. The lights pick shades of blue with a line of green swerving in it. The northern lights preserve to run inside the sky, when hearing the coyotes sing following the steering of mother Earth. Slowly you spot mother Earth going to sleep for the night, which makes you do the equal.

The warm temperature being sent from the solar giving power to all residing creatures as they unsleeping and feed. Placing water onto the night hearth, the leftover smoke filters away just before you leave your region sage in the centre of your stones.

Strolling the day through the timber, you pass the creek wherein mother Earth despatched you the non-secular message. Listening to the facet, you see a toddler black bear in the creek. The black bear seems to be gambling within the water to settle down from the warmth of the sun. The cub was rolling to and fro in the water while having amusing is his personal way. Seeing the black undergo, mother Earth has advised you that super energy and confidence lies inside you.

CHAPTER 3 - RITUALS AND ALSO CEREMONY OF NATIVE AMERICA

Frequently called "religion," most local individuals did now not recall their spirituality, ceremonies, and rituals as "faith," inside the way that Christians do. Alternatively, their ideals and practices shape an imperative and seamless part of their very being. Like different aboriginal peoples around the world, their beliefs were heavily motivated by their strategies of obtaining food – from searching for agriculture.

They also embraced ceremonies and rituals that supplied power to overcome the problems of existence, as wells as activities and milestones, together with puberty, marriage, and loss of life. Through the years, practices, and ceremonies modified with tribes 'desires.

The advent of Ecuador's settlers marked a chief trade in the Native American lifestyle. A number of the primary Europeans that the Indians would meet had frequently been missionaries who looked upon local American Spirituality practices as nugatory superstition stimulated through the Christian Satan. Those early missionaries then decided to convert the Native Americans to Christianity.

Loss of life Ceremonies

Local individuals celebrated demise, knowing that it was a give up to lifestyles on the planet, however, believing it to be the start of life inside the Spirit world. Diverse tribes venerated the useless in several methods, by giving them food, herbs, and gifts to make sure a safe adventure to the afterlife. The Hopi Indians trust that the soul moves along a Sky direction westwards and that those who've lived a righteous existence will tour quite simply. However, individuals who haven't will come upon suffering on their journey.

To make certain a safe adventure, they wash their dead with natural yucca suds and dress them in conventional clothes. Conventional meals and special herbs are served and positioned on the graveside.

The Navajo perceived that residing to antique age turned into a signal of an existence well-lived, as a consequence making sure that the soul might be born again. As a substitute, they felt that if a tribe member died of sudden infection, suicide or violence, a "Chindi, or damaging ghost might want to purpose problem for the own family of the deceased.

Afterlife rituals could last for several days with the cautious idea given to foods and herbs chosen for the celebration, a mirrored image on how the deceased lived their lifestyles. Commonplace herbs used by the Navajo included Broom Snake Weed, cleaning soap Weed, and Utah Juniper.

Many trusts that on that day the spirits return to go to the circle of relatives and friends. In guidance, various tribes could prepare meals and decorate their homes with ears of corn as benefits for the useless.

Rein Corn fairs

Also referred to as the Green Corn Ceremonies, this both a party and religious rite, commonly practiced by means of the peoples of the jap Woodlands and the South-eastern tribes such as the Creek, Cherokee, Seminole, Yuchi, Iroquois, and others. The ceremony usually coincides inside the past due summer time and is tied to the ripening of the corn plants. Marked with dancing, feasting, fasting, and non-secular observations, the ceremony normally lasts for three days. Sports numerous from tribe to tribe, but the commonplace thread is that the corn turned into not to be eaten till the first-rate Spirit has been given his proper thank you.

All through the occasion, tribal individuals provide thank you for the corn, rain, solar, and an awesome harvest. A few tribes even agree that they have been made from corn through the notable Spirits.

The inexperienced Corn pageant is also a religious renewal, with numerous religious ceremonies. In the course of this time, a few tribes hold council conferences wherein a number of the previous yr.'s minor problems or crimes are forgiven. Others also symbolize the event because the time of 12 months when children come of age and infants are given their names.

Numerous tribes include ball video games and tournaments within the occasion. Cleaning and purifying activities frequently arise, including cleansing out homes, burning waste, and ingesting emetics to purify the frame. On the give up of every day of the festival, feasts are held to have a good time the good harvest. Green Corn galas are still practiced today by using many ones of a kind native peoples of the South-eastern wooded area way of life.

Healing Rituals

Symbolic healing rituals and ceremonies had been regularly held to deliver contributors into harmony with themselves, their tribe, and their environment. Ceremonies had been used to help organizations of people return to concord; however, huge ceremonies have been typically no longer used for personal healing. Various widely from tribe to tribe, a few tribes, including the Sioux and Navajo, used a medication wheel, a sacred hoop, and might sing and dance in ceremonies that would be remaining for days.

Historical Indian traditions also used many plant life and herbs as treatments or in non-secular celebrations, developing a connection with spirits and the afterlife. Some of those plants and herbs used in spiritual rituals protected Sage, undergo Berry, pink Cedar, and candy Grass, Tobacco, and lots of others.

The healing system in Native American medicine is a lot exceptional than how maximum people see it nowadays. Local American healing includes beliefs and practices that integrate faith, spirituality, herbal remedy, and rituals that are used for both scientific and emotional conditions. From the local American angle, the medicinal drug is greater about healing the character than curing an ailment. Conventional healers laboured to make the man or woman "entire," believing that maximum ailments stem from religious issues.

In addition to herbal treatments, purifying and cleaning the frame is likewise crucial, and lots of tribes used sweat inns for this reason. In those darkened and heated enclosures, a sick person is probably given an herbal remedy, smoke, or rub themselves with sacred flora, and a healer may use healing practices to power away indignant spirits and invoke the healing powers of others. Sometimes recovery rituals would possibly involve complete groups, wherein individuals could sing, dance, paint their bodies, from time to time, use mind-altering materials to steer the spirits to heal the unwell man or woman.

Peyote Worship

A few southwest tribes have historically practiced Peyote ceremonies, which were linked with eating or consuming of tea made from peyote buttons, the dried fruit of a small cactus, formally referred to as Anhalonium or Lophophora. Native to the decrease Rio Grande River and Mexico, the call "mescal" became wrongly applied to this fruit by many white observers. The ceremonies were held for precise motives, including healing, baptism, funerals, and different special occasions.

Though many have the effect that peyote becomes smoked, this became not the case, because the peyote button will now not burn. As an alternative, the buttons, both sparkling and dried, have been eaten or ground right into a powder and drank in a tea. Rites for those ceremonies might commonly begin in the evening and continue till the subsequent dawn and have been restrained with the aid of some tribes best to men.

Like different Indian ceremonies, fire and incense have been extensively utilized to cleanse the thoughts and frame. The rite also applied hen feathers, which represented hen energy, preferably the ones from predatory birds, which were strong and idea to defend the worshipper.

The ceremonies had been guided through healers, also known as roadmen, as they have been notions to guide a person's adventure through life. Most customarily small drums and rattles have been also utilized.

Referred to as the "sacred medicine," peyote ceremonies are nonetheless practiced these days with the aid of numerous tribes who agree with that it counters the craving for alcohol, heals and teaches righteousness, and is beneficial in combating spiritual, physical, and different social ills. Nowadays, the local American Church is considered one of several non-secular groups to use peyote as a part of its spiritual exercise.

Pow-Wows

A noticeably modern word, the time period derives from the Narragansett phrase "powwaw," which means that "religious leader." earlier than the time period "pow-wow" have become popular, other words were used to describe those gatherings, which include celebration, doing, honest, dinner party, festival, and greater.

The nearest English translation is "assembly." today, it exemplifies all of these events and a cutting-edge pow-wow can be any type of occasion that each local American and non-local American humans meet to bop, sing, socialize, and honour American Indian culture. These events might be precise to a sure tribe or inter-tribal.

Planning for a pow-wow typically begins months earlier of the occasion by using a group of humans generally referred to as a pow-wow committee and may be sponsored through a tribal employer, tribe, or every other organization that wishes to promote Native American subculture. Those occasions nearly usually function dance occasions, a number of that are competitive and might final from hours to numerous days.

Imaginative and prescient Quests

Several local individuals practiced the rite of Vision Quests, which become regularly taken by means of older children earlier than puberty to "locate themselves" and their existence's course. In most instances, the vision quest turned into a "supernatural" enjoy in which the man or woman seeks to engage with a mother or father spirit, normally an animal, to gain recommendation or protection.

A lot of guidance turned into often taken earlier than the vision quest changed into undertaken with the intention to determine the sincerity and commitment of the person. Every now and then the hunt required the character to move alone into the desert for several days, for you to turn out to be attuned to the spirit global. Other tribes required the character to take an extended stroll or were constrained to a small room.

Often the character changed into required to speedy previous to the hunt and was now not allowed to sleep. At some point in this era of sensory deprivation, the character was to search for a guardian spirit's presence or a sign that would be given to them. As soon as the presence or sign was "seen," and the person had realized his/her route in life, they could go back to the tribe to pursue their existence's journey.

Traditional healing

Many conventional healers say that the maximum of the recovery is carried out with the aid of the affected person and that everyone has a responsibility for their right behaviour and health. That is a severe, lifelong duty. Healers function facilitators and counsellors to assist sufferers in healing themselves. Healers use memories, humour, track, tobacco, smudging, and ceremonies to convey healing energies into the healing area and recognition of their results.

The medication Wheel and the four guidelines

The medication Wheel once in a while referred to as the Sacred Hoop has been used by generations of diverse local American tribes for fitness and healing. It embodies the four guidelines, in addition to Father Sky, Mother Earth, and Spirit Tree—all of which represent dimensions of fitness and the cycles of life.

The medication Wheel can take much special paperwork. It is able to be an artwork, including artefacts, or portray, or it could be a bodily production at the land. Loads or maybe heaps of drugs Wheels were constructed on local lands in North America during the last numerous centuries. Movement in the drugs Wheel and in Native American ceremonies is round, and normally in a clockwise, or "sun-wise" course. This allows us to align with the forces of Nature, including gravity and the rising and putting of the solar.

Native individuals have a deep connection to nature that is referenced in assisting establish and keep stability, health and wellbeing. Nature is known as "mother Earth," and due to her importance, she has been adopted into several customs and traditions. One instance of this idea is the medicine wheel, which symbolically represents perfection in addition to the circle of existence.

Maximum medicinal drug wheels, also called sacred hoops, have four not unusual compass points, each with a guiding spirit, that symbolize the four ranges of lifestyles and provide classes and presents that aid the improvement of a balanced life.

Maximum medicinal drug wheels, also known as sacred hoops, have four common compass points, every with a guiding spirit that characterize the four ranges of life and offer lessons and gifts that support the improvement of a balanced life. The four factors may also have animal, plant, celestial, and different representations, which vary significantly from tribe to tribe. For instance, the Buffalo that looks on remedy wheels of the Plains Indians is not represented on the wheels of south-eastern tribes, as that animal turned into uncommon amongst them and alternately an alligator might no longer seem on the drugs wheels of northern tribes.

The number 4 is sacred to many local American tribes because it represents the four seasons, the four human wishes – physical, intellectual, emotional and non-secular. The drugs Wheel can take many different forms in numerous varieties of artistic endeavours, or it is able to be a physical creation at the land. For hundreds of years, remedy Wheels had been built on local lands in North America.

One of the most remarkable is the Bighorn remedy Wheel positioned inside the Bighorn countrywide wooded area in Wyoming. For centuries, this sacred website has been used by Crow youth for fasting and vision quests, and for different local individuals as a website to offer thank you and make prayers.

The drugs Wheel, named through white guys who located it on the quilt of the 1800s, this wheel is stated to serve as a kind of landmark to discover the dawn of the summertime solstice. In its maximum simplistic definition, the medication Wheel is an image of ALL advent, of all races of human beings, birds, fish, animals, trees, and stones.

It has a shape that resembles that of a wagon wheel, fabricated from stones. In step with tribal beliefs, the round shape of the wheel represents the earth, the solar, the moon, and the cycles of lifestyles, the seasons, and day to night time.

There may be an inner circle representing the old female (the earth), Father Sun, Grandmother Moon, and the four factors. Four wonderful rock mounds, set in the four instructions, lay on the perimeter, separated with the aid of stones representing the moon's cycles. Stones, laid from the fringe, in straight strains, to the middle (the spokes of the wheel) represent non-secular paths, leading us to the middle, to ideal stability, to the author.

Prayer to The four guidelines

Incredible Spirit of light, come to me out of the East (purple) with the energy of the rising solar. Allow there to be mild in my words, allow there to be mild on my course that I stroll. Let me consider continually that you supply the gift of a new day. And in no way allow me to be burdened with sorrow by now not beginning once more.

Amazing Spirit of affection, come to me with the energy of the North (white). Make me courageous while the bloodless wind falls upon me. Awesome existence-Giving Spirit, I face the West (black), the direction of sundown. Allow me to bear in mind normal that the instant will come while my solar will cross down. In no way permit me to neglect that I need to fade into you. Supply me a stunning colour, provide me an outstanding sky for placing, so that once it is my time to satisfy you, I'm able to come with glory.

Super Spirit of advent, send me the nice and cosy and soothing winds from the South (yellow). Consolation me and caress me while if I am worn-out and bloodless. Unfold me like the mild breezes that unfold the leaves on the bushes as you provide to all of the earth your warm, shifting wind, supply to me, in order that I can also grow close to you in warmth. Guy did now not create the internet of existence, and he is but a strand in it. Anything man does to the net, and he does to himself.

CHAPTER 4 - HEALING POWER OF STONES

Using sacred stones in healing is a historic exercise relationship back as some distance as our history does. Native individuals utilized the metaphysical strength of the earth's stones to align their power, cleanse the spirit, and improve their physical fitness.

The healing of energy of stones and minerals is all over again, finding recognition as fitness and wellbeing, holistic practices, and non-pharmaceutical treatments are taking the wheel in the international of drugs and well-being. Having been in large part disregarded or forgotten, inside modern-day subculture, stone healing strategies are not exactly a common thing again.

Stones are extraordinarily beneficial in modern technology, their energy being used in the workings of quartz timepieces and energy components inside clever phones and computer systems. They are extensively utilized within medication – minerals contained within stones are floor down and added to pharmaceutical tablets. Simply as a magnet uses its pressure to repel or entice other metals, a stone can be located near different assets of strength and transform, vibrate, circulate and shift that energy according to its very own energetic structure.

So certain stones have specific vibrations and can be utilized to modify the vibrations in us. The right stone has to be selected for the right situation and man or woman, and then the healing possibilities are countless. Our energy and universal fitness all come all the way down to stability. We want to create equilibrium within us with the intention to be able to heal ourselves and live a wholesome existence. The vibrations from a stone emit tiny energy impulses that set off the human body's neurological machine in a diffused manner.

Stone healing is the act of laying on stones (stones and gems) in coordination with the body's energy discipline, energy centres, and energy pathways. Those components of the body's energy discipline also are referred to as the air of mystery, the chakras, and the meridians.

The correct placement of stones at the frame will promote emotional and mental harmony. Its miles on this state that the body reviews the appropriate situations in which to heal certainly. The selected stones and stones have the capability to remove undesirable terrible energy, offer wished healing strength and balance matters.

As well as Stone recovery, there are exclusive approaches to utilize the healing powers of the stones; many people pick out to choose the precise stone and wear it as jewellery or virtually deliver it on their character, or sleep close to them in order that in the course of the night time the energy is handed thru you. Others meditate with their stones or make stone recovery grids, another historical healing technique designed to transmute strength.

How Does Stone recovery works?

Research into the shape of the atom over the previous few hundred years has found out that the entirety in our complete universe is made up of energy. Even strong items, like a chunk of furniture or the hair on your head, are actually just vibrations of energy at the maximum fundamental stages. It is able to not look like it in your eye, but healing stones and the cells to your body are made up of an equal sort of energy.

Scientists have already found out how to use the strength inherent in stones for all types of such things as retaining time the usage of small quartz stones for your watch or growing the electronic additives on your laptop and phone. Whether or not you realize it or not, the energetic homes of healing stones and stones are widely used in our present-day technology. We even use stones in our medications. Many pharmaceuticals are made through ground-up minerals that shape the interior of healing stones. Even though our culture has several uses for the lively houses of stones, we have overlooked to standardize their use in active healing.

When you place positive stones over positive parts of your frame, your strength transforms, vibrates, pulses, moves, and shifts in accordance with the homes and active signature of the stone.

What form of healing can you anticipate From Stones?

You may use stones to heal the whole thing from migraines to anxiety and past. Recovery stones also can boost up your meditation practices, align your seven chakras or even set off trance states below the proper conditions. There's no limit to the sorts or degree of healing you may get from the proper stone or stone within the proper application. If you're trying to heal some issue of your mind, body or spirit, there are essentially 3 number one approaches healing stones can remodel your energy and solve imbalance:

Clearing

Stones have the capacity to absorb and dispose of certain forms of energy from your body. Like a magnet can select up little portions of metallic shavings, a healing stone can soak up bad strength out of your frame.

Energizing.

That is similar to the way energy works through engaging in and transferring energy into an item. A stone can harness strength from the quantum field and ship it into your very own energy subject. Don't fear, in contrast to power, and this stone healing power is painless and not dangerous.

Balancing

Our global is very symmetrical. Look at the leaves on bushes or even your frame. The energy of our planet aligns things in a reflected sample. Every so often, your power may be misaligned and out of balance and healing stones can use the houses stated above, which might be basically attracting and repelling, to stability out areas of energetic disharmony.

Ways to apply healing Stones

There are lots upon heaps of forms of healing stones and stones inside the international. There's a notable amount of untapped recovery energy just sitting accessible waiting for you! However, before we dive into figuring out what sort of stone is ideal on your private use, let's pass over some exclusive approaches you can use stones to heal yourself.

Wear recovery stones. On account that stones and stones soak up, repel, and transmit power, sporting positive recovery stones let you stability your strength subject at some point of the day. Putting to your stone rings inside the morning or placing positive stones for your pocket is like taking your each day vitamin on an active stage.

Everybody familiar with stone healing is probably familiar with this sort of healing—the laying of stones. In case you're looking for a totally direct, unique utility, setting stones on that part of your frame is a great manner to get admission to their healing houses.

Meditate with them.

Healing stones and stones are often tens of millions of year's vintage and that they contain a lot of statistics - our records. In reality, a quartz stone can hold as lots records as over 22,000 iPhones, and that statistics don't degrade over the years. By sitting with stones and quieting your mind throughout meditation, you are often able to intuitively acquire exceptional, existence-changing insights through genuinely preserving an active piece of records like that during your palms at some point of the technique.

Use a healing stone grid.

When you use a stone grid, you precise layout kinds of stones and stones in a predetermined pattern. These styles are designed to get hold of and transmute strength. The usage of a stone grid is an ancient healing approach, and it may take time to study all the different forms of grids. However, the majority locate it to be really worth it as it is an exceedingly powerful exercise.

Sleep near them.

Our conscious minds take over while we're sleeping, and it's a notable time to heal and analyse at an accelerated pace. Permitting healing stones to work while you're sleeping can take away any hurdles, your rational thoughts might be providing with fear or doubt. Try putting stones under your pillow or to your bedside desk and spot how they impact your goals and how you experience when you awaken in the morning.

Pass them across the body. Stones don't want to sit still to work correctly. In reality, every now and then, it's higher to transport stones and stones all around your body to get the maximum healing impact from them. Strive the usage of a healing stone wand to clear negative energy fields out of your head for your toe. Keep in mind that your power subject extends about 3 feet around you, so don't hesitate to works to your entire air of secrecy when practicing stone healing.

Place them in your house or vehicle. You can also use healing stones and stones to guard you or empower a purpose. As an example, you could vicinity protecting stones in your car to block negative energy from injuries or damage INS with the aid of setting that goal into the stone and then leaving in them in the one's locations. You may use them inside an equal manner in your own home or to set the energy for a room. Stones like rose quartz also can draw in romantic energy to your bedroom or healing energy close to your bathtub.

Cleansing and Aligning Your Stones

On account that healing stones soak up, attract and repel certain kinds of power, it's crucial to keep your stones clean. If you use stones to absorb poor energy, you'll want to get rid of that energy before the usage of them once more. Think of this as the usage of a sponge to soak up dirty water. If you need to keep using the sponge, you'll want to squeeze out the dirty, grimy water and easy it up so the following plate you wash doesn't also get dirty.

While you purchase healing stones or stones in a store or online, they had been absorbing and repelling the energy of all and sundry who has touched them. Before you operate them on yourself, you'll need to cleanse their strength and align it with yours.

Healing flora

Native American, Alaska local, and local Hawaiian healers all have an extended record of the use of indigenous, or native, flowers for a huge kind of medicinal functions. Medicinal vegetation and their programs are as numerous as the tribes who use them. Beyond their medicinal advantages, indigenous flora was a staple of native humans' weight-reduction plan earlier than Western contact. These days, indigenous plants are vital to efforts to improve dietary health for current generations.

In Hawai'i, the "Waianae food regimen" and "Pre-Captain cook dinner weight loss plan" aim to reduce empty calories, fats, and components and promote a healthier, greater balanced weight loss plan with the aid of restoring the position of indigenous foods. Alaska Natives and numerous Indian tribes have similar tasks emphasizing traditional foods. In this very actual experience, food is medicine.

The healing benefits of Stones

An increasing number of humanity is re-coming across this historic and often forgotten recovery and recognizing it is a component to play within the recovery procedure. In my treatment technique, as a CTC or Reiki Practitioner, if use the quartz stones above to help enlarge and stability the energy in the room and to assist in channelling ordinary existence power.

There is numerous quantity of different stones on the planet today, but few are utilized in stone healing. The easiest manner to understand the powers of different stones is to examine the homes of colour.

Red

Stones stimulate, spark off, and energize. They're associated with one's ability to use every day practical talents and bodily survival capabilities and with movement, motivation, and safety. Ruby is a terrific example of a purple stone, as it works with the energies of the heart centre, energizing but balancing in its consequences.

Pink

Pink stones have a mild and diffused manner of pushing matters towards a resolution. Pink bestowed on us high feelings and sensitivity to our everyday actions. Rose Quartz is in all likelihood the first-class recognized and favoured of the pink stones, and has a relaxing and reassuring effect. But, it can also be an effective release of unexpressed feelings wherein they may be getting within the way of personal growth.

Moreover, if like Rhodocrosite, a delicate banded stone of crimson, yellow, and orange, to help with enhancing self-photo and self-worth, particularly when issues in this area are preventing motion to your existence.

Orange

Orange stones combine energizing and focusing traits, allowing creative and artistic talents to flourish. Carnelian is one of the more famous orange stones and is characterized by means of a feeling of warmth. Its miles an extremely good stone for increasing motivation, enthusiasm, and energy.

Yellow

Yellow stones can be related to the different body distress like worried, digestive, and immune structures of the body. Amber has a useful effect on the anxious system and self-recovery methods. Citrine Quartz Stone, while its miles a shiny, clear yellow, it's going to assist in preserving the mind clear and cantered. And Iron Pyrites, also called "idiot's gold," allows to cleanse, toughen and calm the digestive system.

Green

Green stones are associated with the heart. They serve to stabilize our feelings and relationships, increase libido and sexual urge, and result in a feeling of calmness in our body system. Green Aventurine is a brilliant heart balancer, and it promotes a smooth expression of emotions. Moreover, this stone is stated to all through the tension and promote a cheeriness in its possessor, and to result in the right luck.

Malachite is going deep, digging out hidden emotions, hurts and resentments, it's going to assist in breaking undesirable ties and styles of behaviour. Amazonite makes a specialty of healing throat and lung troubles. Bloodstone stimulates circulate to the heart, and Emerald will deliver clarity in private courses and calm to the heart.

Light Blue

Light blue stones are related to the throat and, consequently, conversation. Voice, taste, odour, and sight well all of the senses, and your inner communique i.e., the way you speak to yourself, your mind and your capability to explicit yourself, are all inspired by using the vibration of mild blue. Aquamarine is well known for its potential to promote clear communication, braveness, and confidence. It helps you stand your ground and enables you to release the go with the flow of clear communication.

Celestine is a lovely soft stone that paperwork clear, delicate blue stones, very inspiring and dreamy in its features. It is good for lifting heavy moods and assists in the expression of non-secular thoughts. Turquoise dispels any bad strength and electromagnetic smog from your surrounding surroundings, permitting clear wondering and a calming of nerves when speaking in public.

Indigo

Indigo stones are related to your "third eye." Notion, know-how, and intuition, together with a deep sense of peace, are attributed to Indigo. Azurite serves to unfasten up tough and lengthy status blocks in communication and could monitor boundaries stopping us from the use of our full capability. Also, Azurite stimulates reminiscence and take into account.

Violet

Violet stones tap into suggestion, imagination, empathy and the feel of service to others. This particular type of stone helps to rebalance extremes inside the structures of the body so that they can be of use when you aren't certain of the character of trouble. Amethyst is possibly the most beneficial because of the healing stone. It's far universally applicable in its makes use of and blessings.

Amethyst is a great stone to use with meditation because it quietens the thoughts and lets in finer perceptions to emerge as clear. It may decorate intuition and psychic powers of a wide variety. Amethyst is likewise first-rate for lucid dreaming. Also, Fluorite protects against pc and electromagnetic stress, place a fluorite stone at your work station to improve mental readability and efficiency.

White

White or clean stones characterize the potential to reflect all energies around them. White is related to the concepts of readability, cleaning, and purification. Clean Quartz is incredible for strengthening energy. It channels popular power, soaking up, storing, amplifying, balancing, focusing, and transmitting. Because of this, it is beneficial in healing, manifesting, and meditation.
Moonstone is an adorable, gentle luminescent white. It is an extremely good stone for clearing tensions gently from the feelings and from the abdomen, wherein it is able to help the digestive gadget. Moonstone will feature works well

wherever there's an imbalance within the fluid systems of the frame.

Black

Even as white stones replicate and clarify light, black stones take in light. White will reflect the visible, black will display you the hidden potential of any scenario. Black stones are typically grounding, acting as energy anchors that will help you return to an everyday functioning kingdom. Many will even screen hidden aspects so that they may be handled; in this admire, black stones have a purifying function. Smoky Quartz is a gentle grounding stone. It far shielding and is capable of terrible dissolve states. It's going to reach deep ranges of the self to cleanse and balance, and so maybe a beneficial meditation stone.

Local America healing herb

Local Americans trust strongly in the interconnection of all of the introduction. They practice their recovery arts in a way that includes the natural international and the entire person – frame, mind, and spirit. Native individuals accept as true with that illness is a sign of misalignment in the spirit in addition to inside the bodily body.

Addressing the religious nicely-being of the ill is taken into consideration equally or even greater vital than addressing the actual bodily ailments. This idea seemed preposterous to the profoundly Christian settlers; however, it comes complete circle to today's modern-day scientific belief that our emotions.

Lengthy earlier than the Europeans arrived on the North American continent, indigenous human beings have been training herbalism. A number of their understanding of the way flora might be used for well-being came from their eager remark of the natural world around them. They found that deer, elk, and bear sought out vegetation to eat when they were ill. They noticed the animals recover and knew to test with these herbs and flowers to heal themselves

They have been stranded surviving on old rations and simplest rarely consuming a meal of fresh sport. They have become extraordinarily unwell with the sickness that we now understand as scurvy, 25 men died.

Sooner or later, Jacques Cartier met up with Dom Agaya (a local) whom he had visible weeks earlier at which era he had been extremely ill with the same ailment. Cartier locating Dom Agaya now to be in top health puzzled him - what had healed him? He learned that the Iroquois women had brewed him an herbal tea containing juniper bark and needles and had used the tea dregs as a natural poultice for his swollen leg. The French tried this herbal brew and hastily recovered.

The indigenous tribes also laboured and communed with plants and herbs, believing that there has been a trade of recovery facts from the plant life themselves that guided them through the process of choosing the proper herbs and plants for healing. "All plant lives are our brothers and sisters. They talk to us and if we concentrate, we can pay attention to them."

The important strength that moves through the plant world is assumed to be the equal important energy that actions through all of the lifestyles in the world. Flora has been carefully studied by the native individuals over hundreds of years, contributing to the huge know-how base of over 500 natural vegetation. This plant and herbal knowledge discovered and utilized by those early tribes changed into exceeded down orally for the maximum part as little or no became written. Many herbs that were observed and used by local individuals are used today in the ways in which the Native American humans used them.

CHAPTER 5 - WHAT IS REFER TO AS SHAMANISM?

Shamanism is the most historical spiritual and recovery exercise regarded to man. In reality, shamanism and shamanic healing date again to over 100,000 years and had been practiced all throughout the.

The phrase shaman originated from a phrase in Siberia and came to be carried out to medication women and men of indigenous cultures whose practice consists of the flight of the soul. An anthropologist studying indigenous cultures throughout the sector commenced discovering that for different cultures, there have been similarities within the way the drugs males and females laboured with recovery and connecting to the religious aspect of people and the arena.

Even as there have been differences unique to subculture, there have been unique practices that might be found in maximum cultures.

Shamanism is the exercise of these intrinsic strategies, either for recovery or to advantage spiritual know-how. Shamanism must be studied within its cultures, consisting of our current ones. But, the principles of shamanic exercise do now not trade, nor have they changed because of historical instances. The practice was tailored to match the times or the subculture.

So what then is shamanism?

It's far a right away the experience of non-secular understanding. The direct enjoy comes through the strategies inside shamanism, which consist of shamanic traveling. Because of the direct nature of the works, it has a tendency to facilitate an increase in every spiritual religion. Human beings will percentage shamanic reviews in companies, but the insight you gain from shamanic practice are specific to you.

Shamanism's practices usually accompany the perception that the whole thing in the international has a spirit and has to know how to share. This is why you move on trips, to communicate and discover the know-how this is inside different residing and non-living things. Through that, enjoy practitioners of shamanism begin to sense and notice they've interconnection to the sector around them.

As a healing exercise, shamanism has been very powerful for both the people of nowadays and people accomplishing lower back into the beginnings of recorded history. Western remedy seeks to locate one cure that works for many if the wide variety it facilitates is simply too small, it isn't supplied in any respect. The shaman provides a specific remedy, which holistically addresses what someone needs right now.

What are the ideals Of Shamanism?

Shamanism organically arose everywhere in the globe, all at some point in records, as a response to the wishes of humans. Shamanism is an ancient collection of traditions primarily based on the act of voluntarily gaining access to and connecting to non-normal states — or spirit nation-states — for expertise and recovery. The phrase "shaman" comes from the Siberian Tungus tribe. And it approaches "religious healer," or, "one who sees within the darkish."

Typically, there's one shaman consistent with the community. Those shamans access the spirit realm for the reason of character and communal increase and healing. They try this through restoring and disposing of energetic pathways, getting better soul parts, and communicating with non-bodily helpers to discover the religious aspects of contamination and locate answers to lifestyle's apparently not possible questions. This truth-penetrating ability marks them as the sector's very first doctors, storytellers, mystics, or even psychotherapists.

The responsibility of Shamans

Shamanism comes with excellent duty. Alongside truly getting access to those worlds, they have to own the ability to convert what they have learned and experienced right into a concrete change in the physical global. This ability to apply the understanding from the spirit realm as a way to heal and rework the bodily realm is what differentiates shamans from different "religious travellers." for instance, a medium can get admission to those geographical regions, and however they lack physical motion at the same time as there.

As well, a sorcerer may also take motion in an altered country. However, their focus is usually not upon recovery.

Shamans also act as excellent instructors, for the train that everything is lively. They educate that everyone matters are interconnected and alive, including (however virtually now not constrained to) the Earth itself, the celebs inside the sky, or even the wind in the air. For this, it's also the shaman's function in a network to illustrate and hold the harmonious balance of humankind, nature, and spirit.

Despite the fact that shamans in a few methods may also act as instructors, many shamanic healers do now not consider shamanism to be a faith. They feel this way because, inside shamanism, there are no dogmas, no sacred text, and no single founder or chief. When people of non-secular practices may also practice shamanism, and now not all shamans are part of organized religion.

The way to embark on a Shamanic journey

Trance

A shaman can input the spirit realm through trance, which is, in many instances, prompted using rhythmic percussion (a drum or rattle) and/or shaman songs. This is the safest and purest technique of attaining those altered states of awareness. At some stage in those trances, the brain enters the Theta brainwave country. The Theta country exists among being wakeful and asleep. It's where clairvoyance and creativity thrive, and deep religious connection may be skilled.

Plant drugs

Shamans also can be guided in their spiritual journeys with the help of diverse plant medicines. Plant drug treatments are fantastically reputable and typically introduced into focus by means of preceding communication with non-secular entities. But, shamans also report that the vegetation themselves told them of their power.

These flowers contain particularly psychedelic homes and are typically regarded up to as religious entities, themselves — for example, mom Ayahuasca. Some of the more not unusual flora used in shamanic trips are Ayahuasca, Iboga, San Pedro cactus, psychedelic mushrooms (although now not precisely a plant), Salthrough, and Peyote cactus.
Helping spirits

At some point in shamanic journeys, there exist an expansion of assisting spirits. Those spirits come within the form of both spirit publications (humanoid beings) and strength animals (also flowers and insectoids). They take on these acquainted-searching bureaucracy on the way to higher relate with us. Helping spirits manual shamans and spirit vacationers through these different worlds and assist them in healing individuals, the network, and the planet.

Power Animals

Power animals play a key function in shamanic practice. In step with shamanic wisdom, absolutely everyone is born with the spirit of one or more animals. Animal spirits stay with us at some point in our lives and assist in manual and protect us.

They are exceptionally corresponding to the Christian concept of a parent Angel and are vital guides to any challenge undertaken through a shaman. As one movement through existence, they could lose antique and gather new energy animals, depending on wherein they currently want guidance. It's also pretty not unusual for a single individual to have more than one energy animal.

Spirit guides

Spirit publications have a tendency to come forth in those altered states in a human or humanoid shape. They help to manual shamans and spirit travellers through unfamiliar nation-states with ease and comfort — they establish a bond and are very trusted.

A spirit manual is an instructor, a protector, and also a partner. In truth, a few shamans even form a spiritual marriage with their spirit courses. These courses are normally the gods and goddesses of the network, in addition to ancestors wishing to help.

3 Worlds of the Shamanic journey

In shamanic cosmology, the sector is divided into three same elements: the decrease, middle, and top worlds. Those words are frequently symbolized by means of pics of an "international Tree," that's usually called "Axis Mundi."

The roots constitute the lower global. The trunk represents the middle global. And the branches constitute the top globally. It's far the shamanistic trinity. Much like how each part of the tree is important and equal, each world is necessary and equal. Each global includes its personal vibration, information, and strategies of recovery.

During a shamanic journey, shamans should journey between these three worlds to get right of entry to the understanding and healing strategies they want, whether for the man or woman. Typically, a shaman has to journey to the decrease and upper worlds through a type of non-bodily form.

Decrease the world

Contrary to popular assumptions, the decreasing world isn't always one of the shadows and evil goblins — it's an area in which herbal spirits, like our strength animals, vibrate and stay. Its miles in which all factors of nature, from mountains to rivers, to fireflies, can be communed and related with.

One may also experience the decreasing world, as an instance, through transporting to an African-like safari scene, where they will commune with spirit animals of recognizable paperwork, which includes lions and zebras, or mythological — or even legendary — creatures.

Albeit an earthly scene, the ordinary regulations of Earthly physics don't necessarily observe. For that, it's not easy to breathe underwater when dancing with whales, fly inside the sky with eagles, or even experience river rapids on a massive leaf. Being in this global feels just like a terrestrial lucid dream. The lower global is said to be a place of creativity and healing, and, just like a dream, represents the unconscious mind.

Centre world

The middle world is the non-secular size of our bodily international. It's in which our ordinary conscious and waking reality resides. But, it may also be accessed in non-regular states. Such states encompass astral projection and remote viewing/seeing. The non-regular centre world is commonly where a shaman first enters upon leaving their physical frame. It's on this global that they could talk with spirits that stay in this physical truth, along with the spirits of the moon, flora, animals, and dwelling human beings.

But, that is also the sector wherein "misplaced souls" regularly reside — souls which have no longer but been capable of skip over (popularly called ghosts). In truth, because of these misplaced souls, there may be an entire region of shamanic education called "psych pomp work," which goals to assist these souls whole their manner of crossing-over.

The centre world is an intricate one to travel. Spirits met and communicated within this global aren't to be taken critically, as there are really no ethical grounds or standards. Typically, even though, shamans adventure to the middle world to commune with nature (where they generally find out new plant drug treatments) recover misplaced things.

Upper world

The higher international, unlike the Earthly lower and centre Worlds, is abstract, inventive, and different-worldly. It's often known as the "heavens. One may enjoy an inexperienced emerald world with pyramids constructed upon clouds and DNA-searching strands spiralling inside and outside of the stars in the sky.

On this global, spirit courses appear in all styles and sizes: young, ancient, god-like, animal-like, and a combination of animal and humanoid. It's miles wherein big-name nations, celestial and planetary beings, and angels and archetypes will be determined. This international consists of something and the whole thing you'll be able to — and can't — likely image.

A shaman's predominant purpose for traveling the higher world is to commune with spirit publications or spirit instructors. Those instructors help shamans in each divination and in healing. Their know-how teaches of our innermost and truest selves and lets in us to flower into harmony inside ourselves and the extra entire. Shamans visit the upper global to achieve this wisdom. Its miles in which pure Spirit is living, and unlike the centre global, these spirits can — and must— be taken seriously.

These upper world spirit instructors are to offer shamans with their training. From the spirit's attitude, that is a crucial communion as they're otherwise not able to reach bodily, or regular, fact. The top world is said to be the vicinity of our higher selves — of our splendid-conscious that permeates all areas and time.

How Do Shamans understand illness?

With lifestyles, there is struggling within the form of illness. We agree with this. It is microbes, viruses, bacteria, and accidents that motive our bodily body's infection. Inside the equal admire, we trust that it's far ordinarily an imbalance of brain chemistry that reasons mental and emotional illness, such as depression, addiction, and so forth.

They accept as true with that, for real healing, one can't absolutely mask and suppress these outcomes, or signs and symptoms, with medicine. They trust that we should deal with the root cause. The root purpose is something some distance beyond viruses, bacteria, and brain chemistry. The basis motive comes from the inner, non-physical realm: the spirit.

Three reasons for illness

From a shamanistic attitude, there are three traditional causes of intellectual, emotional, and bodily illness:

1. Disharmony (or power Loss)

Either manner, we revel in a loss of livelihood, and that means, and enjoy disempowerment in the system. This lack of will, or life energy, strongly and without delay impacts our active matrix, and might reason us to emerge as quite vulnerable to contamination.

A commonplace, yet tragic, example of this is when there may be an aged couple who have spent maximum in their lives together, and certainly one of them dies. The survivor usually is going right into an existence disaster upon the loss and, rapidly after, incurs an illness (inclusive of cancer) and dies — that's disharmony.

2. Worry

Fear is the maximum commonplace cause of illness. It's responsible for emotions, including tension, strain, anger, jealousy, and so forth. Scientists and researchers also heavily agree that once those strain-producing hormones are present, they fast begin to crumble the protective mantle of the frame's immune machine, as properly because it's an ordinary active matrix.

Illness, as a result, is inevitable. Half of a century ago, the Renaissance doctor, Paracelsus, honourably mentioned that "the concern of disorder is extra dangerous than the disease itself." Shamans would truly consider Paracelsus' findings.

3. Soul Loss

Soul loss is the maximum severe — yet, sadly, still common — purpose of infection. In truth, it's miles the most severe diagnosis and a prime cause of severe contamination and even untimely loss of life.

Soul loss is most customarily skilled after worrying enjoy takes place, including combating in warfare (an all-too-common trigger of PTSD), a bitter divorce, or severe bullying. In a few cases, those reports can be so shattering that one's soul can start to fragment and dissociate. Within the maximum severe and overwhelming instances, those soul elements get too a long way lost and fail to go back.

This all might also seem a piece heavy, that's ok. The factor of all this speak - struggling is to enlighten about healing strategies and no longer the traditional pill-form "healing" strategies that only mask the signs and symptoms, but actual healing techniques that nurture and mend the root of the trouble: the wounded spirit.

What is A Shamanic Healing?

Inside the shamanic perspective, authentic healing religious healing can't be performed on a physical stage. Recovery method to return to wholeness, and returning to wholeness is purely an inside task. It is critical to note that shamans agree with that no matter their brilliant accessibility to the spirit realm, all healing is self-healing. A shamanic healer knows how to flow and manipulate the energy of every other's frame and can bypass know-how through from the spirit realm, but genuine healing needs to take place in the spirit of the character.

Incredibly respected by way of all in their tribesmen, medicinal drug males and females achieved rituals containing chants, smudging, and symbolic dance. These rituals were used to solve any imbalance between top and evil that can exist in the tribe at a given time. The Native Americans believed strongly that awful spirits had been the reason for sickness, dying, and discourse within their people.

In different words, someone has to be inclined and ready to take complete responsibility for their very own recovery there is no magic pill that lies outside of 1's non-secular frame. A shaman may be an excellent tutor, but will no longer deliver all the solutions. It is also crucial to observe that shamanic recovery is not to be a substitute for conventional medical or mental services.

Shamanic healing sessions

As shamanic healing practitioners exist in nearly all cultures, their actual customs may range. They act as a sort of "whole bone," or an intermediary, by means of merging with the spirit realm and connecting with assisting spirits in channelling energies and knowledge to be able to aid in healing within individuals in this size.

The helping spirits of the shamans are capable of diagnosing the reason (due to the fact they are spirit, they can without difficulty see all that is happening at the non-secular stage) of infection, provide perception, and then help to facilitate the desired treatment for recovery.

For that, at some point in a shamanic healing ceremony, the shaman has to move on a shamanic adventure to retrieve this strength and statistics — that is, the middle of a recovery consultation. As properly, many shamans will perform a piece of strength works which will combine the consequences of the adventure, find, and launch blockages, and growth the body's capability to heal. Native American Indians sought spiritual recommendations and healing from the drugs individual in their tribe. These religious healers had a deeply sacred connection to all of the factors of nature. They were visible as mystics, prophets, and teachers.

What takes place throughout the consultation?

Setting

A typical healing consultation can take vicinity inner or exterior, and it is of the purchaser's preference. Whichever manner, the vicinity has to be quiet, safe, and relaxing. A "sacred area" is created.

This area is dedicated to the beginning, releasing, and recovery. Consequences such as a candle show, incense, or Palo Santo (holy wood) burning, an altar with stones or special stones, soothing track, and a comfortable location to lie down on are commonly covered.

Open communique with Shaman

The first component so as to happen is an open discussion among the patron and the shaman. For this, the shaman will maintain a decent, non-judgmental space. They'll speak the customer's history, and/or how their soul is feeling at the present second. The shaman will encourage and encourage the client to dig deeper into their tale and, without a doubt, open up as they each hunt for truth and healing capacity.

Those conversations are typically handy and efficient, as the shaman is skilled in fostering and nurturing that secure space, and the patron is inclined to be obvious with the intention to heal.

Active work

Subsequently, they circulate into the ceremonial works. Right now, the client can lie on their back, wearing free and secure apparel. The shaman will then determine their diverse power centres (commonly discovered alongside the seven chakras of the body). At this point, the shaman can feel where pointless energy is being stored, in which stagnant energy may be released, and wherein empowering energy may be located.

The Shamanic adventure

When the strength works are whole, and the shaman will then describe to the customer what they may revel in the course of the subsequent part of the consultation: tingling and warming sensations, meditative-like states of attention, and emotional launch, and/or the energy of the spiritual communion itself.

Even as on this non-bodily trance, the shaman can also do both hands-on or arms-off energy work, through channelling power from the spirit world and moving it in the course of the client's frame consequently. This portion of the rite usually lasts - an hour.

The return

As soon as the shaman has lower back from their adventure, they are once more ready to preserve space for dialogue. Right here, they may talk with the purchaser what become skilled (on each end), what information and advice turned into proficient to them from the spirit realm, and what the purchaser can then begin implementing differently of their lives so that it will heal.

Integration: an essential Step

Humans often sense adjustments and shifts in their energy. Though it is among the healing technique. Toxins which have lengthy been stored in the bodily, mental, emotional, and religious body are being launched. Its miles the shaman's greatest recommendation to pay attention to and take delivery of the lively changes one may experience following a consultation. Any soreness will pass, and new, vibrant life strength will take its area.

CHAPTER 6 - SHAMANIC PLANT MEDICINE HEALING CEREMONIES

The second healing exercise differs greatly from an average recovery session as the consumer goes on a spiritual adventure.

Remedy men might turn to their medicine bag, and its contents to treat anything was ailing a member of their tribe. Gadgets found on this sacred bag are nevertheless used these days in rituals and spiritual ceremonies. Things like candy grass braids, witch hazel bark, white sage, Echinacea, and incense have been all quintessential elements in the healing rituals performed by using the medicine women and men.

With deep meditative techniques, non-normal geographical regions can be accessed using shamanic trance-inducing strategies. In this way, one may be completely present and on top of things. But, there is any other route you'll take to gain this healing and access these non-normal states: plant drug treatments. The difference is that the plant is the vehicle wherein one is riding round in, and every plant has its own specific manner of touring those worlds.

Misconceptions of plant drug treatments

In the latest years, the curiosity of many humans within the Western world about indigenous cultures and their plant medicines have peaked. This latest interest, but, has been accompanied by the misconception of the medicine, the revel in supplied, and its gigantic healing houses.

In the shamanic way of life, these flowers are not tablets. As a substitute, they're exceptionally respected sacred drugs. They agree that the flowers can show us non-normal nation-states where know-how can be attained, growth can be extended, and authentic healing can take region.

How are plant medicines traditionally used?

Those plant drug treatments need to be skilled in a ceremonial context with an educated shaman. The shaman's job at some stage in one of these ceremonies is to enrol in the client in his or her adventure, keep a secure area, manual, guard, and intervene if needed. The Shaman also facilitates the customer to later interpret, recognize, and combine their experience. One ought to experience called — no longer forced — to participate in a plant remedy ceremony. You need to be geared up to make a bodily, emotional, mental, and spiritual alternate.

One ought to also be ready to absolutely give up to the plant and let it take them where they want to go. The plant spirit always is aware of precisely what one most desires to peer, sense, hear, experience, and, consequently, research. Because this vegetation is so powerful, they regularly seem through shamanic cultures as religious entities or Gods and Goddesses.

Many common shamanic plant drugs include, however, are truly not confined to Ayahuasca, Iboga, San Pedro cactus, psychedelic mushrooms (although now not exactly a plant), Salthrough, and Peyote cactus. To provide a quick evaluation and an example of what a plant medicinal drug rite is, we can take a short look at the (presently) most famous of these plant drug treatments, Ayahuasca.

Ayahuasca

Unlike other sacred plant drug treatments, Ayahuasca is comprised of separate plant life: the chacruna leaf (Psychotria Viridis) and the Ayahuasca vine (Banisteriopsis caapi). Alone, neither of these plant life produces medicinal nor entheogenic homes. But, when combined, they work together and emerge as a very powerful and sacred medicine.

Each of these flora is located within the Amazon rainforest in South America. And in this unique rainforest, there are over eighty, 000 leafy plant species. Yet, someway, the psych pharmacologists of the Amazon (the shamanic healers) knew exactly which two unsuspecting plant species might create this kind of magical and psychoactive medication when mixed.

Shamanic Healing

Shamanic healing addresses the non-secular thing of contamination. Shamans believe that infection/damage seems on this spirit earlier than it shows up within the physical body. Shamans trust that healing on the spiritual stage can save you conditions from performing in the body, and also that healing the spirit allows or lets in the body to heal once a condition has regarded.

Unlike western remedy, the way the religious infection affects the frame isn't usually the same. The way to address the same circumstance can be absolutely exclusive from one client to the subsequent. The "one approach/one pill treatment options all" idea doesn't do works in shamanism. There is a mysterious detail about how the shaman affects a therapy.

Healing VS healing procedures

Shamanic healing has effected treatment options on many exceptional forms of situations. It's far capable of addressing any illness. The healing takes place on many ranges: within the feelings, inside the frame, in relationships with others, and in courting to the planet.

Therapy is one dimensional, you have an illness, and a therapy eliminates it. Treatment options do no longer address your sense of properly-being or whether your existence is wealthy and full of strength.

Shamans are seeking to perform healing, which might also result in cures. Shamanic works has and keeps to provide remedies, however, is hard for a shaman to say to you 'yes if will therapy your such and such condition.' every now and then a shaman will discover that he/she is right at a particular remedy, however for the maximum component you may most effective discover if shamanic healing will work for something particular with the aid of trying it.

Please word, a shaman must never advise that his or her recovery can take the region of western medication. There's no motive that shamanic works cannot be done together with western remedy. A moral shamanic practitioner could in no way recommend you surrender your doctor or your current treatments. You need to constantly visit your physician in case you sense changes that want to be made to your present-day medical treatments.

In the local American Indian subculture, a few healers also had the ability to result in visions. These humans were known as shamans. The maximum skilled of all healers, the tribal shaman, became capable of input a deep trance that connected them to the underworld searching for recovery. Those bright and severe desires added the shaman to a better state of reality.

Illness as a teacher

No shaman wants another to suffer. (As constantly, those are descriptions of shamanic practitioners inside the satisfactory experience. it is possible to satisfy unethical practitioners, and also you need to take care to interact with a truthful healer.) A shaman does the works due to a preference to ease your manner, and out of trying the quality for you.

But, maximum shamans understand that illness can be a superb instructor. In fact, its miles the shaman's very own illnesses / difficult times that have created an open and compassionate coronary heart. It is this compassionate heart that allows the shaman to heal.

A shaman knows a way to be with you while you are struggling due to his or her own instances of suffering. Consequently, a shaman will not count on that curing your contamination is the quality element. As a substitute, he/she plays recovery to your maximum accurate. That means that in preference to forming preconceived notions about what's quality for you, the shaman lets the spirits / God / the universe make that choice.

There are numerous individuals who have had a few contaminations and claim that it helped them learn something they wouldn't have recognized or to acquire something. Through working through the contamination, it may have taught them how to persist in different areas of their lifestyles. A shaman can in no way make sure whether or not curing someone could intervene or assist.

Due to the fact, a shaman can't be certain of the solution to such questions, he or she will no longer assume what's first-class for you. Rather the shaman places out a name to the healing forces inside the universe. It's far a call that strongly says 'heal for this customer's highest suitable.' This healing then may also deal with something emotional, it could cope with something physical, but it is always supposed to present you extra spiritual power.

Documented instances exist of individuals being cured of cancer, blindness, and other seemingly unbeatable contamination through shamanic remedy. You may acquire one of these healing, and the extra you can open yourself to that opportunity the more you will allow the recovery forces to be available.

Your very own healing powers

Whenever a scientific look is completed to check a medicinal drug, there's usually a collection of folks that receive the actual medicinal drug and a collection who get hold of a placebo. The placebo is not the drugs but is a sugar tablet. A placebo is used because there may usually be a few members so that it will show development or treatment regardless of whether the drugs are effective. So a percentage of the humans inside the placebo group will improve despite the fact that they have got not been given "real" medication.

Is it because of the scientific attention the affected person receives after they partake in a look at it? A shaman's explanation for this will be that belief in the placebo helped the man or woman engaged along with her personal energy to heal herself. In other words, the affected person recovers at the placebo due to the fact he is connected along with his very own energy of self-healing.

What will engage that healing motion within you?

That is, an element, what shamans are looking to interact, your personal healing skills? Shamans truly do work on the religious stage, clearing out blockages and returning misplaced energy. However, one of the aims of healing is to connect clients with the power this is inner themselves. This energy may be used to enhance one's life in numerous ways, including coming from a powerful place as you interact within the private global or the commercial enterprise world, being a writer in the global, and being the healthiest human you could be.

Shamanic Extraction

This is a process that work side by side with the spirit or the soul and that they work with strength. Within the case of shamanic extraction, they are operating with misplaced energy. No energy is honestly terrible from a shamanic attitude.

If energy is misplaced or it isn't in accord with the surroundings (the human frame, or the frame of land, it will deliver contamination. Shamanic extraction is the removal of displaced energy, on occasion known as intrusions. This is a strength that does not belong in the body and might motive the infection.

In which area does mis-placed energy come from?

All of us are conscious that emotional states can impact health. The strain is mentioned to reason backaches and ulcers. Shamans consider that your emotion takes the form of power and may be stored at some point in the body and ultimately result in illness. So you keep your pressure or anger in your stomach.

Otherwise, you get irritated and ship your anger out at a person. We can see this if you can recall a time when someone's anger or unhappiness appeared to have an effect on a room: "her anger hit me like a blow" or "you may reduce the tension with a knife."

The strength that can be stored within the frame does now not must be from anger; however, maybe from different motives as nicely. In the shamanic mind, there's no difference made primarily based on where the energy came from. The shaman sees that the strength does no longer belong there and eliminates it.

Other sorts of out of place power will be the energy left in the back of from harm. A person sprains his/her ankle, and a lively injury may also continue to be that may perpetuate weakness in that vicinity. Shamanically, everything has a soul, so the heart transplanted from every other might also nonetheless comprise energy from the organ donor.

This power may or might not be well suited to the heart transplant recipient. If it's now not, the shaman could dispose of the 'displaced' strength. This is including the body's rejection of the heart so that the rejection could be less intense... As it does no longer belong there, it reasons contamination or weak point inside the frame.

The Extraction: finding and eliminating the misplaced strength

The shaman will first enter a shamanic nation of recognition to diagnose and locate wherein misplaced energy is probably in the body. This transformation in attention permits the shaman to peer in a different way, to peer what is going on energetically.

The shaman will understand the energy in a few manners in an effort to illustrate to her or to him that it wishes to be eliminated. It may seem to the shaman as black sludge, or as an attacking snake, have a scent, or be felt as heaviness. The way each shaman perceives that there is out of place energy varies; however, there may always be a signal of a few kinds which says 'this doesn't belong here.'

Once the shaman has located the misplaced power, he or she will then merge completely with their father or mother spirits or energy animals. Merging with recovery spirits will increase the shaman's power and allows them to do away with the energy. It also protects the shaman from taking power into her or his very own frame for the duration of the shamanic extraction.

This growth of strength permits the shaman to drag the energy out, as though he or she has a more potent magnet to tug with. If the shaman will increase the power of his or her magnet sufficiently to overcome that strength's preserve on the body, it is able to be eliminated.

Relying on the shamanic practitioner and the character of the displaced energy, this could be a very quiet process. With a few practitioners, the extraction may be pretty a show. The shamanic practitioner merged with an energy animal may flow further as his or her power animal. She or he may also make the sounds of the strongest animal.

As an instance, if the animal is a snake, the practitioner may also hiss when eliminating the energy block. In case you are interested in having an extraction, you could discuss this together with your shamanic practitioner.

Sound contraptions can be used, consisting of a rattle or a drum, to boom the energy or the energy of the "magnet." The shamanic practitioner can also sing to hold her or his shamanic state or to increase his energy at some stage in the process.

The shamanic practitioner will dispose of the eliminated energy in various approaches. She may also transmute (transform) the energy right into an extra-fine lifestyle, improving strength. He may also location it in water and have the water neutralize it. Once the extraction is executed, the shamanic practitioner will fill the void in the customer's frame that changed into created by way of the vacated energy. The practitioner can also update it with healing strength, carry out a strength animal retrieval, or perform a soul retrieval. The shaman will not go away a void for different energy to fill.

Protecting your self

In your frame, there is numerous issue you could do. To guard yourself against out of doors energy, you may imagine you're self-surrounded with the aid of protection. One generally used approach is to ascertain you're self-surrounded by using a translucent blue egg that lets in simplest tremendous power in and lets in power again out.

This may surround you as you go - your each day life. If the environment is intense or someone is combative, you could wish to consider a brick wall for that time. Click on for extra facts on energy safety.

When you are feeling negative emotions, it's miles important no longer to disregard them, or they may get stored in your body. They want to be expressed and allowed to depart your frame. You do not need to ship them to others both. You may request that as you specific your emotions, they may be converted into more neutral or healing energy with the aid of the universe or your mother or father spirits. You could visualize the emotions flowing into mild and becoming brilliant and clear.

There are stones, or other items that are can absorb terrible power. If this appeals to you: Heavy or leaden stones are idea to soak up strength. Examples are granite, galena, and hematite. There are stones that transform and lighten energy consisting of selenite, calcite, and quartz.

A darkish purple amethyst can serve as a great protective stone. Moldavite will transform the negative into superb and has been acknowledged to get bodily warm at the same time as doing so (this stone is expensive but.) you could have the stone on your pocket, put on it as a pendant, or location it at the desk wherein you figure.

People who interact on this practice will smooth their stones with water, or vicinity them in a sunny window to clean up any energy that could get stored in the stones. (Selenite does now not want to cleanse.) If you feel your stones want a more radical cleaning, they may be buried outdoor to be healed with the aid of the earth. Stores that sell these objects are regularly indexed under "Rock stores" in the yellow pages. You may seek the internet for 'rock and mineral stores.'

As you drink water, believe it was filling your body while remodelling the out of place power. Or you may cross swimming and believe this. Layout in the sun and imagine it melting away your intrusions and filling you with glowing healing strength. Simply make sure to imagine something changing that is eliminated.

Soul Retrieval

The free Soul

The human soul is free to depart the body. Shamans trade their kingdom of consciousness, allowing their loose soul to journey and retrieve historical understanding and lost strength. Due to the fact, the soul is free to go away the body, and it's going to achieve this when dreaming. Or it'll depart the body to shield itself from unfavourable conditions, both emotional and physical. If the soul doesn't come returned on its personal, a shaman should intrude and return the soul essence.

Motives for the Soul's Departure

There are various motives for soul loss, all of which are wholesome approaches to protecting yourself:

- Someone becomes in an abusive state of affairs, and the soul left to protect itself from the abuse.
- A toddler would possibly have sent his or her soul to hide while his dad and mom have been fighting.
- The soul may jump out of the frame just prior to a twist of fate to keep away from the pressure of the accident.
- A person near died, and the soul left until the person is ready to cope with his or her grief.

Again, all of these are healthful mechanisms of protection. But if it does now not realize how to return, or doesn't realize it's secure to – the shaman may also want to help them go back that missing piece.

When two human beings are in love, or while they may be in a family, they'll provide an element in their soul to their cherished ones. A mother can also provide a few to her baby due to the fact she desires to shield her or him. A lover might also deliver part of his or her soul to stay near

This form of soul alternate may also seem good enough because you need to share yourself with another. It's far usually now not a good idea, however. No one can use every other individual's soul, as it isn't always their soul. The one that you love has to deal with unusable power further to his or her very own troubles.

We don't recognize we are doing this soul sharing, because we had been by no means taught about it. As you end up a greater awareness of it, you could discover more empowering approaches to sharing love and affection. You may see the language of soul loss in regular speaking. You would possibly have heard a person say she "misplaced a chunk of herself" while she parted with a lover, or the x-boyfriend announcing "you stole my lifestyles from me."

That is one-of-a-kind than a person supplying you with their soul; in this situation, you took it for a few purposes. Soul stealing can be harmless, and you notice a person with masses of power, and also you want to borrow a number of it. You are fearful of dropping a person so that you take a chunk of that person with you, so you will usually have her or him close by.

Soul stealing can be visible where an abusive partner has taken his or her accomplice's soul. When you are taking a person's soul, you take some of that individual's strength.

Its miles critical to realize that nobody can take your soul without your consent. It might have been regular for your family to borrow energy from every different. Or you might not have found out it was ok to say no. If, for a few reasons, you sense that someone is tugging at your soul, make a firm selection within yourself that they can't have it, and they will now not be capable of taking it from you.

Signs and symptoms of Soul Loss

Soul loss might be much like the psychological idea of disassociation. Another time the language of our society refers to soul loss, I lost something when I lost my job, I never felt the identical after my coincidence

Some of the signs and symptoms that would imply soul loss to a shaman include:

- Depression
- Feeling incomplete.
- Incapacity to move ahead on some problems.
- Lost recollections.
- Feeling like you're not in control of your lifestyles.
- Folks that say I felt like a part of me died while
- People who say I sense like so-and-so stole my soul.

Soul loss is regularly accompanied by way of a sense that something is lacking from life. Coma is a situation of excessive soul loss. In a coma, extra of the soul is out of the frame than in. As with the opposite shielding feature of soul loss, this will be very appropriate. If the frame is in a super deal of ache, or if the soul wishes time to don't forget its situation, a coma offers wished time. Shock is some other symptom of soul loss, in which the individual's soul hasn't back but or hasn't completely re-entered the frame.

So if the soul component was lost to a person, or in a specific region, a character might also experience an urge to return to that location or person. Once in a while, while someone has a suicidal mind, it could be due to a preference to reunite with one's misplaced soul pieces.

The Soul Retrieval procedure

If a shaman healer discovers anything in your soul, he will decide if you need a soul part returned. Then the shaman would take any other adventure to retrieve any soul portions that should come lower back presently. Within the practices taught within the US, and in lots of components of the sector, the shaman brings the soul pieces returned with them from his or her adventure. The healer would then blow every piece lower back into the frame of the consumer, one at the time, focusing in order that the soul essence fills that character's frame.

In maximum instances, you may need a healer to perform the soul retrieval for you. It's not easy to do that for yourself. Also, a vital element of shamanic healing is the love that is felt while someone plays a healing for you.

However, a few approaches to try this yourself encompass, requesting the souls go back:

- Putting the query to the universe.
- Praying.
- Inquiring for a healing dream.
- Asking your father or mother angel or parent spirits to go back soul portions to you.

It is virtually in the power of the individual to launch any soul parts they will have due to soul sharing. See underneath for more statistics about liberating elements you are keeping. Don't neglect the importance of having a person carry out a soul retrieval for you due to the fact you feel you have to do it for your personal. Its miles crucial to be lively in one's personal healing.

However, an energetic part is normally essential once the soul is lower back to you. The soul retrieval itself could be very tons about receiving, so whether you engage the assistance of a shamanic practitioner or not, don't forget about this important thing.

This area is one where you're held in a field of love, and one which protects you from the interferences of the outdoor world. If you come to be vulnerable for the duration of the soul retrieval, the shamanic practitioner protects that vulnerability. It isn't clean to do that for oneself, -and- carry out the soul retrieval, -and- drum, -and- be receiving, you get the concept.

The Soul's return

In indigenous cultures with lively shamans, you would now not be without your soul portions for very lengthy. The soul retrieval healing would frequently be accompanied by the party or a joyous welcome from the circle of relative's members. In nowadays subculture, but an entire lifetime can move by way of earlier than certain pieces come domestic.

However, you feel it, and it's essential to rejoice the return of your critical essence lower back to where it belongs – inside an equal manner, we might have a good time the return of a protracted misplaced cherished one.

Humans' reactions after their soul retrieval are very various. Some people feel amazing pleasure, some humans sadness, a few human beings feel fuller, a few people sense lighter, some human beings experience nothing there is no 'one' or 'proper' manner.

Some of the advantages that have been skilled by using humans who have acquired a soul retrieval include:

- A more capability to make selections of their existence
- A feeling of being more present in their lifestyles
- The capacity to transport skip a difficulty that previously could not
- The start of a brand new increase or healing technique.

A potential to start managing grief

A few healers will tell you what gifts your soul is bringing lower back to you. As an example, go back to your capability to have the wish or confidence in yourself. The practitioner is unable to forecast for you what will be the result of the process. However, it is also know that it will begin the works of the latest healing and new growing.

It's essential to be open.

Openness facilitates you fully acquire your soul element back, and lets in you to notice something new you need to convey into your existence.

Possibly you want to have more a laugh to satisfy the needs of the lower back piece of yourself, and perhaps you need to move outdoor more.

Perhaps you want to provide yourself a length of introspection after the soul retrieval has occurred. Perhaps the soul retrieval became just the final of a missing piece for your healing process. You need to care for yourself as you would a new-born and supply yourself anything you discover is needed now that this present has back.

In case you are uncertain about bringing up soul retrieval, you may constantly tell them you experience like you reclaimed part of yourself recently and aren't sure what to do. Therapists keep in mind that idea no matter whether or now not they agree within soul retrieval itself.

Finding the right Healer

You need to pick someone who performs soul retrieval often. When you are sure he or she has the right revel in, the next maximum important component is how you sense about the healer. When you are looking for someone to perform your soul retrieval, it's far vital that you feel secure along with your desire.

Folks who recognize the way to consider themselves aren't possible to have any issues locating the right practitioner. If this is a subject of yours, right here is a few data about choosing:

Locate someone who has the proper knowledge in shape with you.

If you don't feel relaxed with a practitioner, it doesn't matter that their call got here particularly encouraged by way of someone or if they may be especially skilled. A few people are in shape better with positive practitioners than with others. An awesome practitioner will be very accepting of you, and judgmental language is a caution signal.

Returning Soul parts which you are retaining:

Going outside, getting a spray, and snapping it in half of to signify which you would love to release the souls you're maintaining. You may take an item inclusive of a quartz stone that represents the person's soul and deliver it to the individual as a gift.

Talk a request that your father or mother spirits go back to the soul pieces you are keeping. Its miles best essential for you to send a clear message that you want to launch the soul portions, so something method that appears suitable for you may work.

In case you are definitely inclined to release the soul piece, that is. In some cases, it's far hard to let move while someone is now not in our existence, together with a lover we've broken up with. You can need to first do the work of being inclined to release what you are retaining of them. Possibly you're unwilling to let go of the manipulation. Don't decide yourself, but instead, try and get to the lowest of why you are preserving on. Remember that it makes your existence extra difficult while you attempt to preserve on.

How Do I recognize if I need a Soul Retrieval?

Many human beings recognize that they're missing something. But for the one's individuals who aren't so properly connected with their intuition, they might not have that consciousness. As cited above, signs/indicators of soul loss can consist of:

- Emotions of depression
- A sense of being incomplete
- Submit stressful Stress Syndrome or PTSD like signs.
- Inability to move beyond a problem despite efforts to accomplish that.
- Feeling such as you've performed the whole lot you could do but are still caught.
- Feeling disconnected from existence, like you don't, without a doubt, feel whatever, or you feel you couldn't hook up with things.

- Reminiscences or incident on your beyond when you can say, I feel that I misplaced something that I in no way were given returned.

- An experience that a person took part in you, your coronary heart, your soul, or that you have been not the equal once they left you or died.

- You hold wanting to go back to someone, or a region that appears dangerous or not likely, even though there's no apparent cause for you to achieve this.

It isn't important with the intention to have a severe symptom to indicate soul loss. It's miles truly real that a few human beings have experienced blessings, even though they had been not positive whether they had soul loss or no longer. If you experience this is something you may want to attempt, that may be the right reason to contact a practitioner. They could go on a diagnostic journey to discover if this will be fine for you at the moment. If you aren't in a place wherein you are ready to try this, it may be suitable if you want to wait.

The following blessings are with soul retrieval, although there's no assure what is going to appear, all soul retrievals are one-of-a-kind:

- You may find it less complicated to move forward on an issue that has been troubling you.

- You may experience a sense of what you're really seeing your life for the first time. You can locate it easier to make certain selections or make certain adjustments.
- You can discover that some features you have got struggled with inclusive of hopelessness, lack of confidence, anger may also enhance or prevent absolutely after a soul retrieval.
- You can locate that you can hook up with matters more effortlessly.
- You may sense an absolute extra gift. It is usually for the subsequent demanding situations to be introduced up with soul retrieval.
- You may have feelings of unhappiness or depression due to the time that went by means of missing this a part of you. Problems that you have formerly been unwilling to address can come to the floor
- You can locate that you may now not live in a scenario which you had been dwelling with – such that you find you have to make adjustments for your lifestyles.
- You can discover feelings that you previously did no longer wish to cope with assert themselves, which includes grief or anger.
- You may begin a protracted healing technique.

There may be no understanding of what may also manifest because of the end result of soul retrieval. In some cases, someone may also actually reports a complete flip around of their lifestyles, to a greater happy manner of being. In some cases, it starts off evolved a procedure of adjustments that take time to fully emerge. And of the route, some humans feel that no longer plenty absolutely occurred as a result of their soul retrieval.

Your instincts have to inform you what to do, and the practitioner allows you to decide if a soul retrieval would be helpful to you at the moment. However, have a sense of worry due to the fact it's far unknown, you could usually touch a practitioner to virtually speak soul retrieval or your fears.

See the way you experience after you have discussed it with him or her, and then determine whether or not you wish to continue.

Sooner or later, an advantage of soul retrieval or any shamanic healing is when you consider that someone cares enough that will help you. Most shamanic practitioners feel a strong choice to assist in making your avenue a touch less difficult. A few human beings say that this is the maximum benefit a part of the healing process for them.

Lengthy Distance recovery process

Time in space is similar and very essential in the Shamanic belief. People who practice shamanic techniques regularly find that many stuff may be finished in a quick period of time. And people regularly return from their shamanic trips with wonder at how "it regarded like it was long gone longer than that" or "I didn't suppose I will go that long."

Time and space also are taken into consideration relative to science. (Which means no longer set in stone however flexible and changeable. we could say compressible.) However, we don't need to go into Quantum Physics here, so we'll sum it up that the shamanic journey can take benefit of those principles because in the adventure you aren't sure to the guidelines of matter/the physical form, but can alternatively observe the policies of strength. When on a journey first-rate, "distances" can be crossed speedy. Time can expand or agreement, so you can accomplish what is needed within the time available, and the shaman can visit in which he or she is needed.

Long Distance healing

In an extended distance recovery, a shaman healer will adventure to wherein you are, and perform a healing on you in a comparable manner to what they might do if they have been proper there with you in bodily form.

Human beings may or might not have sensations while this healing is taking place, depending on the person's sensitivity. Also, because time is relative, the individual being healed may not receive the results of the recovery within the second in which the shaman is performing the healing.

Healing such as soul retrieval, shamanic extraction, energy animal retrieval, in addition to any wide variety of healing, can be performed at a distance by way of the healer for their customer. The healer might also truly send recovery energy to the person. Recovery can be despatched with the aid of a collection of human beings to a person, in a comparable manner to how a group prayer is accomplished.

Does it work?

Regardless of whether or not it makes sense to our everyday questioning, long-distance healing is mentioned to work well. But there is a giant amount of humans who have suggested powerful recovery consequences once they have acquired lengthy distance healing. It also ought to be noted that shamanic healing is not the best healing modality that makes use of lengthy-distance healing. Reiki, as an instance, utilizes long-distance recovery.

Many lengthy distance healers will nation somewhere that they provide this provider. However, you could continually ask. Some healers specialize in long-distance healing simplest. As with any healing, use your own judgment while deciding on a healer for lengthy distance healing.

Why long-distance?

Finding a healer close by. Long-distance recovery offers the capability for a man or woman who is in a much-removed area, or a vicinity wherein such healing services appear unavailable, to receive healing from a shaman irrespective of the distances.

It also permits an individual to obtain healing from a shaman that they especially want to work with. Using long-distance recovery also can be applied in situations when it isn't always appropriate to have a healer in the identical region because the person being healed or directly touching the purchaser.

Such as though the man or woman to be healed has a contagious infection, cannot be touched for some purpose, or feels more at ease with the long-distance approach. Long-distance healing is frequently used with animals, who are occasionally unwilling to sit down still long sufficient to be healed.

This fact must be made cleared that there are certain advantages that can be lost in a long-distance recovery. When a shaman healer plays healing in person, they invent a sacred space for you.

They may be there to support you immediately on your healing method. There are numerous appropriate reviews about lengthy distance healings, so it's miles possible that some healers nevertheless create this helping space for their customers no matter the distance. You have to usually experience loose to speak about your wishes and worries with a potential shamanic healer.

CHAPTER 7 - THE HISTORY OF AYAHUASCA

The records of Ayahuasca use dates thus far lower back that anthropologists and researchers have yet been able to trace its origins. But, the shamans claim that the flowers, themselves, informed them for the duration of a middle international shamanic ages.

The plant life is accumulated from the jungle and brewed right into a sacred tea. The tea, when taken ceremonially, throws open the gates to the spirit realm and famous mystical, non-everyday worlds, which might be unperceivable in everyday cognizance.

Traditionally, it became handiest the shaman who would drink the Ayahuasca brew. They could do this to be able to induce their shamanic journeys at some stage in a healing session and convey expertise and steerage again, which will help in healing individuals and the community.

Modern-day uses of Ayahuasca

Presently, the use of this brew has undoubtedly advanced to attain more and more human beings. Now, any interested person (no longer just an experienced shaman) can experience the first-rate healing energy of Ayahuasca. Alas, many Western cultures have not begun been capable of absolutely understand the recovery and medicinal residences of this precise plant substance. Yet, in the Amazonian nations of Peru, Ecuador, Colombia, Bolithrough, and Brazil, Ayahuasca is each criminal and relatively celebrate

It is throughout these ceremonies that individuals are able to face the root reasons in their physical, intellectual, emotional, and spiritual illnesses head-on and delve deep into the healing procedure by way of allowing the spirit of Ayahuasca to take them on a journey to these states of non-regular consciousness. Within those realms, problems that have long been hidden in the subconscious thoughts are revealed. Mom Ayahuasca will continually train the player exactly what they most need to learn how to completely, without a doubt, heal themselves.

An Ayahuasca ceremony

As precise traditions inner Ayahuasca ceremonies will range from shaman to shaman, those following customs normally live the same:

Education — Ayahuasca eating regimen

Ayahuasca is a complete spirit, mind, and frame cleanse. To put together for the revel in a unique weight loss plan (or diet, as it is commonly mentioned in South America) is pretty recommended.

Typically, at a few degrees inside the primary 1/2 of a rite, there's an honest quantity of purging from both or each end. That is due to the fact Ayahuasca is purifying the bodily frame of pollution earlier than it movements directly to highbrow, emotional, and religious frame purification.

A way to lesson, or, in some instances, definitely keep away from, the purging method is to start the purification manner the week in advance than the ceremony. Unique diets range know-how commonly requires one to abstain from capsules, alcohol, and processed additives.

A few times, diet even requires the absence of intercourse, salt, meat, spice, and sugar. In loads of cultures, respecting and following a diet is paying an extremely good homage to mom Ayahuasca.

The rite

Each shaman has their very own manner of putting in the ceremonial location. Maximum ceremonies are held after sundown at ease, a laugh, a comfortable environment. In fact, many take region inside the lively confines of the Amazon Rainforest.

The shamans create a completely open and at ease space by lighting fixtures incense and candles, putting in place altars, and gambling soothing percussion. She or he is probably able to also smooth and guard the energy of the space through filling the room off, and blowing onto the crown every player, a shape of sacred tobacco referred to as "Mapacho," as pictured above.

Then, the shaman expertise that virtually absolutely everyone set a cause for his or her journey whether or no longer that be to floor past wounds or to observe self-love. The organization then prays together and gives way to Mother Ayahuasca.

Ultimately, one after the other, every participant drinks the brew and begins off-evolved to journey. As quickly as the drugs kick in, the shaman will begin to sing icaros, or shaman songs, which assist in intensifying the medication and further shield the strength of the room.

The pass lower back

Ayahuasca commonly lasts around five hours. As every person inside the rite starts off-evolved to return to waking, conscious truth, the shaman will again use Mapacho to clean the power of the distance and ground absolutely everyone. The ground will then be open for sharing and heartfelt communion. The shaman will then assist in mixing their revel into the bodily fact, and offer recommendation on expertise include their newly found into their lives for maximum beneficial healing.

Why do human beings Use Ayahuasca?

In traditional cultures, it's frequently used by shamans or medicine men to open up the verbal exchange with nature. Those non-secular leaders also use it to determine what's inflicting someone to be sick on the non-secular degree. In a few religious ceremonies together within Brazil, ayahuasca is taken by using everybody who participates within the ceremony, and they sing and chant as they float right into a trance.

In cutting-edge Western society, there is a hobby in ayahuasca by using those who are intrigued by the use of thoughts-changing substances to overcome fears and discover the talents in their thoughts.

Humans also often become a hobby in ayahuasca after listening to anecdotal testimonies of people who've used it to heal an expansion of troubles, which include addiction and depression. Of path, this isn't the simplest psychedelic that's been used for that cause.

How does it work?

People are frequently fascinated no longer just in the memories and myths surrounding ayahuasca, however also in understanding how this mysterious tea works on the mind.

Within about a 1/2 hour after consuming ayahuasca tea, human beings revel in something that they describe as hallucinations. People who have used it don't sense adore it's similar to an experience they may get with LSD, but, and that they describe it as extra emotional and spiritual, in preference to being recreational.

There have been mined scans showing using this tea can lower interest in positive regions of the mind. Those areas, after they're overactive, are associated with situations like anxiety and social phobia as well as despair, so it stands to cause that this is why human beings sense like consuming ayahuasca is probably beneficial for those issues. The DMT component of ayahuasca is also related to proteins that assist with reminiscence and the regeneration of neurons.

Regularly some of the human beings that are probable to apply ayahuasca are operating through a substance abuse trouble or addiction, alcoholism, or depression. A few people who are improving addicts or who have experienced the trauma of their life say that the usage of ayahuasca tea has helped them works through these situations and heal themselves, although this is, of the route, subjective and tough to a degree.

Is Ayahuasca legal?

You'll be questioning is ayahuasca legal, especially given its similarities to psychedelic tablets that clearly aren't criminal inside the AMERICA

First, there's the DMT component of ayahuasca tea, without which the substance wouldn't have the identical effects. DMT is unlawful quite much universally around the world. However, the actual plant resources it isn't.

This has led numerous human beings to purchase vegetation that incorporate DMT online, which isn't always technically illegal in most locations. The exception simplest happens in a few countries like France, where they have got outlawed all flowers used to make ayahuasca.

This would mean in technical standards, DMT is illegal. Consequently, ayahuasca is circuitously illegal. The ayahuasca brews using DMT are illegal inside the AMERICA, but there's work through certain spiritual agencies to the mission this. They're the use of arguments similar to what befell with the local American Church and the use of peyote.

There had been a few courtroom cases that have allowed sure groups to import ayahuasca tea to the AMERICA for non-secular ceremonies because of rules just like the spiritual Freedom Restoration Act.

There have been comparable conditions in different countries. For instance, inside the mid-1980s, the religious use of ayahuasca turned into legalized in Brazil.

Despite various and regularly vague legal fame of ayahuasca tea in the AMERICA and around the arena, many people have become to vacations as a manner to attempt the substance. Writers from outlets like national geography have written about their journeys to South America, and the big apple instances included it in 2010.

Folks who go to ayahuasca retreats in the Amazon rainforest regularly cross for the healing of each mental and bodily illness, and there may be a chunk of statistics showing it may enhance fitness.

To sum up, the query is ayahuasca legal—in the AMERICA, the tea itself isn't necessarily unlawful. However, the vital DMT element is, as DMT is a time table I drug

What's Ayahuasca Tea?

Ayahuasca tea is an herbal drink that combines flowers observed evidently within the jungle of the Amazon, and it's been in use for hundreds of years as part of religious and recuperation ceremonies. Proponents of ayahuasca tea sense that it has healing advantages, and it reasons hallucinations. Western medicine has been paying attention to ayahuasca for the potential of the tea to help people who be afflicted by problems like depression and anxiety.

The use of ayahuasca tea has come to be so popular that the whole tourism industry has advanced round it in South America since one of the essential ingredients, DMT, is an agenda I substance in the AMERICA and is illegal in many different international locations.

The tea will also be blended with the leaves of a shrub called Psychotria Viridis, or depending on the country the tea is being made in, other shrubs can also be mixed. Ayahuasca tea is blended with a plant species that incorporates DMT, which in the instance above, is the Psychotria Viridis.

Physical Ayahuasca results

First and principal, one of the most prominent ayahuasca side results is vomiting, and diarrhoea may also arise. There are individuals who welcome this side effect, feeling as its cleansing and permits them to purge the terrible from their lives. In truth. There are people who have defined the vomit as coming in buckets and as "natural hell" with regards to ayahuasca, and for a few people who take this substance it is able to show up very quickly after consuming it, and for others, it can manifest in the midst of the hallucinations.

Other side results of ayahuasca that stem from the whole from the usage of the DMT factor of the tea encompass extended heart fee, dizziness, agitation, accelerated blood pressure, dilated students, chest pain, and in high doses, extreme side results like seizures. DMT intoxication also can lead to high blood pressure.

Psychological Ayahuasca consequences

Alongside the physical ayahuasca consequences, some of the effects of the usage of this substance are psychological. As with other psychedelic tablets, while you operate ayahuasca, you may revel in hallucinations, and while human beings frequently see them as religious or healing stories, it's vital to recognize there's no manner to are expecting how you will react and what your revel in might be like. This is the problem with such a lot of hallucinogens that people don't bear in mind.

It doesn't matter what number of tales you've to examine - the profound enjoyment of ayahuasca and DMT because you can have a specific revel in.

Some human beings say they felt severe anxiety, paranoia, and worry, and it is able to convey up past traumas and be very unsettling for many people. These are a number of the feelings that therapist's sense could link the usage of ayahuasca to having psychiatric value, but if you're not insecure surroundings with individuals who are trained within the use of the substance, it may be very dangerous. It could turn out to be a frightening revel in that many people aren't prepared for.

Critical Ayahuasca outcomes

It's also crucial to realize that every other potential risk with the use of ayahuasca, and greater mainly DMT, is serotonin syndrome. Serotonin syndrome is most probable to occur in folks that are taking antidepressants. Different potentially deadly dangers related to ayahuasca and DMT consist of seizures, respiratory arrest, and coma. In human beings who've pre-current mental problems like schizophrenia, there also can be intense facet-consequences while using ayahuasca.

Is Ayahuasca Addictive?

The real drug DMT itself isn't presently recognized to have a capability for physical dependency or dependence, but what can show up is a psychological craving. This is something that's seen with other hallucinogens as nicely. Even as the chemical make-up of DMT won't lead to addiction, people often end up psychologically addicted to the using of a drug like DMT or consuming ayahuasca tea. Humans may also want to get away their reality or have a reference to different people that can come from the instances surrounding ayahuasca.

To this point, there haven't been any big studies regarding the use of DMT therapeutically, and there's just restricted scientific and medical studies universal when it comes to ayahuasca consequences.

It's essential that human beings recognize with limited studies and information, unregulated use, and the dangers that come with hallucinogens in general that the usage of ayahuasca isn't something endorsed. There are such a lot of unknown variables, from what happens when you're using the drug, to the potential long-term results.

CONCLUSION

Most shamans have desires or visions that deliver certain messages. Those spirit guides are usually the notion of being present in the shaman, although others are stated to come upon them handiest while the shaman is in a trance. Shamans declare to heal inside the religious dimension by way of returning lost parts of the human soul from anyplace they have long gone.

Shamans claim to benefit expertise and the power to heal in the religious world or dimension. Most shamans have goals or visions that carry positive messages. Shamans might also claim to have or have obtained many spirit guides, which they consider guide and direct them of their travels in the spirit world.

Those spirit guides are always thought to be present in the shaman, despite the fact that others are said to come upon them handiest when the shaman is in a trance. The spirit manual energizes the shamans, permitting them to go into the spiritual dimension. Shamans claim to heal within the non-secular dimension through returning lost elements of the human soul from anyplace they have got gone.

An account states that the gifts and payments that a shaman receives are given by way of his companion spirit. Since it obliges the shaman to apply his gift and to work regularly on this ability, the spirit rewards him with the goods that it gets.

Those goods, however, are only "welcome addenda." They're no longer enough to allow a complete-time shaman. Because of the popularity of ayahuasca tourism in South America, there are practitioners in regions frequented with the aid of backpackers who make a residing from main ceremonies.

This is a popularly found in the amazon vicinity, and it's a psychoactive drug due to the reality it can create altered states of awareness. When a person takes ayahuasca, the outcomes can vary quite dramatically from one individual to the next, and one revel into the next one. For example, a few human beings can use ayahuasca and just find that it's a bit stimulating, while other human beings report having extreme visions.

The primary component of ayahuasca, that's taken as a tea, is a vine. The vine is also referred to as ayahuasca, and it method vine of the soul or vine with a soul. Those teas also produce other ingredients, which include the chacruna plant, which also has a psychedelic substance known as DMT. Even as the tea is called after the vine element it's made with, and it's the DMT that creates the experience such a lot of humans associated with the usage of ayahuasca.

The name of this root and tea originated from the Quechua language, which is being densely spoken in region like Ecuador, Bolithrough, and Peru. There are also distinct names for the brew based totally on unique groups of people. For instance, in Peru, the Sharanahua people name it shori.

Printed in Great Britain
by Amazon

24376364R00089